BLACK RITUALS

BOOKS BY
STERLING D. PLUMPP

Portable Soul
(poetry)

Half Black, Half Blacker
(poetry)

Steps To Break The Circle
(poetry)

Blues: The Story Untold
(poetry)

Black

Rituals

by

Sterling Plumpp

wTp
THIRD WORLD PRESS, Chicago, Illinois 60619

DEDICATED TO:

Haki Madhubuti, Falvia D., Murry DePillars, Johari M. Kunjufu, Safisha Madhubuti, Calvin Jones, Soyini Olamina, Jabari Mahiri, Chaga Olamina, Harold Hunter, Sharon Scott, Margaret Neal, Virginia Johnson (one and two), Sharon Thomas, Julius MacAllister, Herchel Hunter, Cecil Curtwright, Henrietta Collins, Hoyt Fuller and Imamu Amiri Baraka

With poems for haki and murry

CONTENTS

CHAPTER ONE
INTRODUCTION

       IN WRITING THIS BOOK ON BLACK PSYchology, I realize that I'm breaking all taboos in this society; I'm taking my life into my own hands. Let me be very clear about something; I'm not a psychologist though I've studied psychology for over five years; I'm a poet. I sense my world; my own experiences are as valuable to me, as reliable to me as anything in the universe. Thus what I'm doing in *Black Rituals* is forcing coherence, order, structure on all the experiences I've had with Black People. This book is written to clarify the psychological position Black People are in now at this critical juncture in our history.

    This book is about Black Survival; I'm writing to expose those habits of thinking which don't facilitate Black advancement, and to suggest what would do so. I seriously regret that America, the United States, has produced no Black psychologist relevant enough to aid me. I mean somebody in Fanon's bracket. Of course, we do have the serious scholarship of Dr. Kenneth B. Clark, but the main thrust of his effort has been to show the oppressor what he is doing to the oppressed, and not to show the oppressed how to successfully deal with his oppression. Occasionally, Dr. Alvin Poussaint has donated scholarly articles on topics, but his work lacks overall cohesion, vision. Then we have Cobbs and Grier, two psychiatrists, whose *Black Rage* and *The Jesus Bag*, were, I hope, spurious attempts to capitalize on anything Black while there was commercial value in it. Grier and Cobbs said less in their two books about Black People than most kindergarteners could say with chalk and a blackboard. The major problem with their work is that it is unscientific; but even worse, they lost the golden opportunity to adequately describe Black People. Anyway, Fanon is the only Black psychologist who could've been relevant to me in the writing of *Black Rituals*. But his major works are more relevant where the solution to the problem of the oppressed is violent dialogue with the oppressor. I don't rule out that option for Africans in America, but if it comes to that, then Fanon has adequately analyzed the processes. What I must deal with is the transitional period where Black People must organize/unify/mobilize to seize enough power within the system so later phases will be able to occur.

Black Rituals is a book dealing with the problems the Black Man must face if he continues with his present methods of relating to the world, and the problem he will surely face if he changes. Thus my book is primarily descriptive, but it is also historical because I use my own life as a referent point. I cannot separate my life from that of Black People. What I say of them is true of me. My approach has been to open my own entrance into Black Rituals, then to analyze the consequences of Black Rituals for Black People, and to end by again talking about how change came to me as a function of change that came to Black People generally.

CHAPTER TWO

DAWN OF MY MIND:
A PROLOGUE

I REMEMBER VERY VIVIDLY THE NIGHT I got 'ligion and jined church. It was in 1951, and the Mississippi July was hot and humid as ever; the sun was up sparkling down its beams before six when I got up, and was flowing gently behind formidable woods after seven in the evening. All the crops had been laid by, the horse and cattle pastured, and everywhere Mother Nature gave evidence of her role as Nurturer: Lima and Butter Beans were twirled round poles as if in some fierce amorous embrace, potato vines covered the head of the ground, and watermelons could be seen resting quietly amid a tribe of grass. It was the time of year when people go fishing, visit friends, or wade in the serenity of shade trees. I was happy and spent much time swimming in the ponds and lakes within a ten mile radius of my house. I had been told about God, Christ, and getting saved all my life but now that I was eleven, just one year before I would become responsible for my own soul at the age of twelve, I was prime target for those holy ad-men of the Lord whose sole function was to get the lost to come to Revival Meetings. Momma had been trying to get us to go to Sunday School for some time and we had made personal contact with a Sunday School teacher by cutting her grass, pruning her peach trees, and doing general handy work for her.

The immediate impetus to my getting converted was not the Black Church but a Revival sponsored by a Reverend

Younger, a white Evangelist. Every year he had black children remember verbatim a chapter from the New Testament as the key for their admittance into Summer Camp. In 1951 it was First and Second Thessalonians. I had trouble remembering every word and I didn't have any clothing suitable enough to wear to the occasion. Fortunately, a black friend of the family was also a friend of the reigning Revivalist and interceded for me, and I went to his house and was given all the clothing that would fit. The occasion marked the first time in my life that I had entered the front door of Mister Charlie's house. And it was also the first that I had ever really had any Sunday clothes. I got several pairs of shoes, two suits, ties, shirts, and, of course, a Bible. The son of the minister, Bobby, sealed the deal by being very friendly. In fact, when the Minister brought me home, he and I sat on the front seat and his two little daughters sat on the back one.

Revival wasn't my first introduction to Black Religion; it was merely my first lesson on the rhetoric of Black Rituals, for I had been bathed in Black Religion since the day I opened my eyes. I knew that there was an omnipotent God who made the rains fall, an omniscient God who knew what was best, and that there was an all-forgiving God who would forgive all who bowed to their knees in submission to His Being. My grandfather and grandmother went to church every Sunday, read the Bible to us, talked about how good God was, and prayed aloud to Him at night before they went to bed. They even taught us a prayer:

> Now I lay me down to sleep
> I pray the Lord my soul to keep.
> If I should die before I wake
> I pray the Lord
> My soul to take. AMEN.

In fact, our whole home was run like a sort of mundane Heaven; Poppa was the all-powerful and all-knowing God, and Momma an angel supporting him. We, the children, were angels when we were good and did something that pleased Poppa, and devils when we dabbled in mischief and displeased him. Our punishment was our banishment from the heaven of his praises to the lowest depths of hell where his razor strap was the final arbiter.

Revival Time was a time of intense spiritual duress for me. I had always thought whatever I did was natural but when I found out that doing what one wants to do conflicts with the Savior's Plan, I became despondent and sought ways to defend what my life had been. The architects of the Revival had an airtight case against me as a sinner; I would have to admit my sins, accept the Christ and be baptized into a new way of life. It wasn't easy. To sort of catch me off guard, the Revivalists held spontaneous watermelon contests where we Black children were lined up and given slices of watermelons; at the word "go" we began eating as fast as we could until only one diner remained. Our pictures were taken. The results were bellyaches, soiled clothing, and much laughter. Often the watermelon eating contest was followed by impromptu prayers or songs.

In the evening before we left our barracks and made our way to the meeting place, supper was served; we had as much as we wanted. Normally, we went over in groups; the boys together and the girls together.

But naturally, there was mating among us. The ones most experienced at attending Revival Meetings had learned the trick of slipping off into the solitude of the woods. The sinners sat in the front rows of the auditorium and the Evangelist and his cast manned the stage of what was our assembly room during school days. A memorable feature of the Revival was the Williams Singers. I can only remember Miss Josie Pearl Williams who played the piano and was the lead singer. It was her screaming voice, leaping up through the ceiling, dancing out the doors, calling, beckoning the lost, that made me feel my deep need to be saved. Every night Sister Josie Pearl ended the meeting with "Oh, If We Never Meet Again," crooning, "I know God will be with us/if we never meet again." Somehow, I wanted to meet again, and one night after many testimonies, yes Lords, and songs, I followed the line of those who had accepted the Lamb. I was perspiring madly and could barely keep

13

from screaming out in jubilation, but I merely walked up to the Reverend and knelt with him as he prayed and thanked the Lord. My grandmother was out there among the happy faces and she gave me spending money after the event. The night I accepted the Lord is a night I still never forget for I felt a relationship with everything. I could start all over and walk the steps of righteousness. I looked forward to the day I would be baptized and jine church.

My conversion was my first step in accepting the formal Black Church because after summer camp, Holy Ghost Baptist Church held its Revival and I went regularly to the meetings. One night my cousin and I went up to the preacher when the "Sheaves" were being brought in and told him that we had been saved during summer camp and wished to be baptized and jine his church. I lived in grave anticipation awaiting my baptism. I was as light as a feather and Momma and Poppa asked me if I knowed what I was doing and I told them yes'um. They told me I could be baptized but that I would have to go to church and Sunday School every Sunday. They said that they would give me money to pay my dues. My life took on a very structured manner, getting up early, shining my shoes, and walking down the dusty roads to the church for Sunday School and Church Service later.

Baptism was on a late Saturday evening in Lake Kickapoo. I wore a gown made of a corn meal sack. I trembled in fear for I had heard of embarrassing incidences where the elect on their maiden immersion into the rite of holy initiation had nearly strangled from the dive. I didn't want to cause a scene. I walked slowly to the edge of the water to a cadre of baptismal ushers who comforted neophytes before leading us out into the cool water about waist deep. After the Reverend had raised his right hand into the sky to beckon down the Holy Spirit, he placed his hand over my eyes and bent me backwards into the waters and brought me back up very abruptly. My weak frame shook and my wet gown stuck to my body like the wrappings of a mummy. I was ashamed and cold as I was led away to a nearby shelter to dry myself and dress. The entire evening after my baptism, I felt relieved, cleansed, chosen. I was very conscious of my words, walks, and ways. I carefully laid out my attire for the following day, shined my shoes, and went to bed early, for on Sunday I would be receiving the Right Hand of Fellowship and the Lord's Supper.

I was sharp as a tack as I sat in Sunday School the next day. All of us new converts suddenly found ourselves the equals of the veteran Christians. We were very enthusiastic during the class and everybody was quick to congratulate us with a smile, a handshake, or a pat on the shoulder. After Sunday School we meandered from group to group receiving the praises of the grown folks who were scattered on the lawn of the church during the interlude between Sunday School and Church Service. Older people wandered in by ones, twos, and threes—older people who didn't go to Sunday School anymore but always managed to make Service. In fact, Poppa and Momma, members of Mound Hood Baptist Church, made it to the various sessions of talkers before church service began.

Gradually the grown folks and then the chilluns drift into the church and take seats. The chilluns sit up in the front and the grown folks in the back except for the Sisters, who have special places for them set aside up front on either side of the pulpit. The choir is seated up front. In the pulpit, there was a rostrum with a huge family Bible on it. Sitting around in circles like the Knights of the round table are the pastor in the center, his son and various other pastors close to him, and the many, many jackleg preachers sitting farthest away, on the outer perimeter.

The service begins with a prayer by one of the jackleg preachers who does his thing for about ten minutes. Then immediately following, the whole church, along with the choir, sings "Every Time I Feel the Spirit." After this, the "Welcoming" is given by one of the select Sisters, the Scriptures read by one of the visiting pastors, and another song is sung—probably, "Some Glad Morning When This Life Is Over." The pastor then rises and reminscences about his childhood and when he was saved; he jokes with the circle of preachers and congratulates the Deacons and Sis-

15

ters for their service to the church; he tells the new converts how fortunate they are that they have had the chance to seek, see, and accept the Light. Then he thanks the Lord for everybody in church for fifteen minutes.

The pastor then breaks in with his favorite, "Give Me That Old Time Religion" and the ushers parole the aisle with collection baskets. A few Sisters let out shouts of happiness but the song ends before the spirit really comes over anybody. The son of the pastor soon rises and tells about how understanding his father has been, forgiving him his trespasses, and leading him down the road to the Servant-hood of the Lord. He then reads a text from the Old Testament; then he repeats it, then he asks the congregation a question which he answers. As the preacher leads the congregation to the very stairs of the Last Judgment, his voice is no longer the voice of a speaker, but the voice of a chanter; his words come very fast, yet they come in a very rhythmic manner.

Suddenly, when happiness makes him close the Bible and leave the pulpit, hopping from side to side in the outer perimeter of it, he chants his sermon and the deacons and brothers begin chants of "AMEN," but the other preachers merely sit with their legs crossed nodding their heads. Soon the Sisters begin to chant with him, parts from songs are interjected into his sermon, and soon one Sister jumps up crying, "Oh Lord" and stands with her body quivering, but her lips are still. The female ushers dressed in white saunter around her, and to the tune of "It's okay, sister," they waltz her toward the door for some fresh air. The pastor and the Sisters preach for forty minutes and the sermon is followed by a song, "This Little Light of Mine." After this, the main collection is taken. The loaded ushers walk toward the Treasurer and he announces that only three dollars are needed to make one hundred dollars; then he announces that only three cents are needed to make one hundred and ten dollars; then he announces that only fifty cents are needed to make one hundred and fifty dollars.

The formal initiation into Black Religion is the "Right Hand of Fellowship" ceremony; all the new converts stand

*in a circle and all the members of the church go around
them shaking their hands. The whole thing takes about
thirty minutes and your hands are sore after the many,
many hand-squeezes and sincere admonishments.*

I felt honored during my initiation because all the big
shots talked with me, even the pastor clad in a black suit,
white shirt, black tie, black shoes, and cleanly-shaven head;
his teeth were sparse with the two front ones being covered
with gold. When the pastor laughed it came from the depth
of his being like cool waters coming up from a deep well; he
told me that he and my grandfather had been boys together
and that he knew both my mother and my father and that
he had been to my house and had eaten on many occasions.
I was very happy and knew I would feel at home when I
went to church instead of feeling like an accused killer waiting for some dreadful verdict. Later, after my initiation was
over, I got my first taste of the Lord's body and the Lord's
blood; it was really yeast bread and grape juice.

Conversion changed my life greatly because my actions
were controlled by guidelines which I was responsible for.
Before I jined church I wasn't twelve and therefore was not
responsible for the fate of my soul. I found that I felt guilty
whenever I broke one of the Lord's Commandments, and I
really thought my soul would be hellbound if I deliberately
defied holy laws. I gradually learned to fear the Lord and
never to mock holy things or be disrespectful to old people.
It was hard for me, and much of the carefree, natural joy
I had known earlier left me. I began to worry more about
the state of my soul than about the state of my body. I
gradually learned to say "if the Lord is willing" whenever
I stated that I intended to do something in the future. I was
always told that tomorrow wasn't promised to me and I
walked with cautious steps. But the newness of conversion
wears off after about six months and you begin to feel that
playing ball all day long, shooting marbles, hunting birds,
or going off into the woods on Sundays are more important
than going to church and Sunday School. In fact, only the
"young men of promise" kept their appointments at the
Lord's Temple; we others went sporadically, and found our-

selves in frequent consultations with our parents and with the spiritual overseers of the community.

The longer I was a Christian the more my interest fluctuated with the rhythms of the seasons; I looked forward to fall because I always had new clothes to wear and I could also see the new converts sitting on the mourners' bench, being baptized, and finally being initiated into the Lord's Temple; winters always found me ready to go to church because it gave me an opportunity to see classmates that I saw five days a week at school, and it also gave me something to talk about at school the next week; in spring I was interested in church until my shoes lost their soles; and, summers were always boring because it was hot and the pleasure of Nature was too much competition. Even when I did not go to church on Sundays I felt something was going to happen to me for not doing so; if I fished I thought I would catch something that would swallow me whole; if I swam I thought I would surely drown; if I climbed trees I thought I would fall; and if I walked down the railroad tracks I thought some fast train would run me down without warning. I could never get away from the law of the Church. Finally, my irregularity at attending and my laxity in paying my dues forced my name from the roll call. I was slipping from the King's Highway and didn't know how to get back on the right trail. But every night before I went to bed I got on my knees and asked the Lord to forgive me for my sins; I didn't want to die in a state of unforgiveness.

As the years went by and I entered my teens, the Lord's message continued to come to me through the words and ways of my parents; they always paid tribute to the Lord and had faith that He would stand by them no matter how great a trial they had to go through; and finally when the boat of life had wandered long enough over rough and tempestuous seas, the Lord would take the ship home and there would be much rejoicing. I have never wanted to die, yet I rejoiced when my parents rejoiced because I saw the same happy, near ecstatic, yet serene expression on their faces when they talked about the Goodness of the Lord and being with Him that I had witnessed in them when they were genuinely gay, laughing, eating watermelon, or watching tall, green corn, with its tassle and ribbons flowing to a cool afternoon breeze. I walked under the shadow of the Cross during all my younger years and no matter how far I strayed from the road of righteousness, I always knew how to fall upon my knees and thus avoid eternal damnation. I never wanted to challenge Nature, though I wanted to be a part of it. I never doubted the validity of Black Religion as long as I was a part of it; I just knew that the laws of the Church were the right ones to live by. All through my life old people had died, young ones were killed, and babies born all because it was the Lord's Will. I had no notion of statistics and could not analyze the births, deaths, etc. . . . on a statistical basis. I was conditioned to bear hardships when they came and to rejoice when goodtimes came. I grew up aware that I didn't have absolute control over my life and I knew that if I wanted to be happy and live to be an old man, then there were certain rituals that I had to perform, and they all had their origin in the Black Church. The whole Black Church's spirituality became so much a part of me that I could never quite free myself of it. I will always believe in a spiritual dimension of life because so much of what I know was experienced at the spiritual level. I learned by sensing before I was taught that I could conceptualize the world, operationally defining it in material terms. My earliest reality was cloaked in a very, very profound mythology.

I never knew how ingrained Black Religion had been instilled into the marrow of my being until I became a convert to Catholicism at the age of fifteen. I was lured into the Catholic Church because guardian angels, Holy Eucharist, Confession, and purgatory led to a foolproof way of gaining eternal life. But long before I had finished my instructional and probationary period, I genuinely missed the preaching, singing, and shouting of the Black Baptist Church. Somehow I always felt that the Catholic Church was too rational, too proper, and I never felt anything in it; I always went through their rituals and hoped for the best, but when I went to Black religious services, I knew that the Lord had been present and had touched me. There was always a rhythm in the Black Church paced by handclaps, footstomps, yes Lords, Amens, nods, and shouts, that made me know that religion was something experienced, and not something learned logically; you felt religion. My shift from Black Rituals to White Rationalism also created other problems for me. As long as I was under the guidance of Black Rituals, I never questioned the circumstances of my birth and I could've become a preacher if the Lord called me. But within the Catholic Church the Lord didn't call young men, they decided that they wanted to enter a seminary; however, bastards needed a special diocesan dispensation to enter, and I was a bastard. I wanted to become a priest because I thought the Lord told all young men "to go and sell what thou hast . . . and come and follow me." I didn't have anything to sell but I wanted to follow Him.

My sojourn in the Catholic Church was a five-year disappointment because I was always doing something which didn't go to the essences of me; I wasn't faking but I was never moved. I was outside of my culture and consequently a stranger, and didn't know how to deal with the fact. I became a picture Catholic, an altar boy: Mass and Communion daily, rosary daily, and Confession weekly, but I never had the same feeling of salvation that I had felt when Sister Josie Pearl sang "Oh If We Never Meet Again." I never thought Catholic priests preached, merely that they read and talked. I never got used to the organ, and the kyries, Christes and agnus deis never replaced "Every Time I Feel the Spirit" and "Swing Low, Sweet Chariot." Deep within my heart I felt that I had betrayed my people as long as I was a Catholic—not that I really found the answers to my life in the Black Church and Black Rituals—but I definitely wouldn't find them in the Catholic Church; besides, my parents weren't Catholic and I didn't make my First Communion at six but at fifteen.

When I graduated from high school and entered college at the age of twenty, I began my comeback trail to Black Rituals. I had the fortune and misfortune to win a scholarship to St. Benedict's College in Atchison, Kansas. The experience a Black man undergoes in a predominately white college with only ten or so Negroes there is enough to drive a rock insane. The only thing that could save me at St. Benedict's was Black Rituals and all I could get was the Blues. I bought several Lps by Ray Charles and I again got the religious feeling I had known as a child. Through them I found strength enough to remain at St. Benedict's for two years. Those two years of college and priests who drank as much as Dean Martin made me doubt the validity of Catholic teaching. I began a serious reading of everything written by Black writers after my sophomore year. I left Kansas and came to Chicago to the Main Post Office where I witnessed more life than I had read about in all of those books. W. E. B. DuBois, James Baldwin, Richard Wright, and Ralph Ellison made me know that something was special about the experience of a Black Man born in America; he had a special vision and could see what others couldn't. DuBois, Baldwin, and Wright made me seriously doubt the necessity of religion, even doubt that God existed. What I thought was a rebellion against Black Rituals and the Catholic Church was merely a reaction against what I had been taught; I had never defined for myself what religion is, what or who God is, and who I was, and it was this process of the birth of my mind that made me call myself an atheist. I had no other label to place upon myself, but I was no atheist for I was desperately trying to find answers about God; if I had been an atheist, then I would have had the answers—God didn't exist and that was it.

Quite another change came over me when I spent two years in the Army from 1964-1966 because I had grown older and had read more about other religions, particularly, Buddhism and Hinduism. I also read Sartre, Camus, Kirkegaard, Henry Miller, and Arthur Miller and the thing I found out about religion, reality, truth, and life was that everything depended on how well the individual evaluated his own experiences. Thus I ceased calling myself anything and started to play music that really moved me—jazz, rock-and-roll, gospels, spirituals, blues, and sermons. I re-discovered in the Army just how religious I was at my base and I accepted the fact. I no longer equated Black Religion with the confines of a church building and I knew it was a source of power within me. When I started to write, it was the spring of my experiences with the Black Church that gave energy and direction to my efforts. I'm religious and Black Rituals are as much a part of me as my hair, my eyes, my ears, my soul, but I've been taught various rational ways to conceptualize my experiences and I can verbalize what I feel. When I left the Catholic church, and after that the silly belief that I was an atheist, and returned to an acceptance of Black religion on my own terms, it was the dawn of my mind, the awakening in me of an unnoticed sea.

CHAPTER THREE

BLACK WOMAN:
EVE OF AGES GONE

When I look into your face
Green conjure Trumpets
Play Africans meadows to me
I hear Sheba sowing her graces
And her wise odors
Strangely lift me from the ground
I know the rhyme of your throes
Your agony peals in my every heart beat
And I taste your chimes
When I breathe
Even before you became a Mammy
Your were Catholic Mother
Dark Deep Sea of All Life
Sometimes in your honey brown eyes
I see pyramids rise
Hear Shaka's footsteps Sense the innocent
Power of King Tut Taste Shango . . .
I have known you for ages
As you danced to Wine Wells
In the late evenings and took upon your head
Our rich sweet beverage of survival . . .
I have seen you walk barefooted
Through dew through burning coals
And on sharp thorns to bring the next
Generations forward

Your voice, the Mystic Oracle
Of the Universe, has blessed my ears
With seasoned tones . . .
I have seen you slender and rhythmic
As the dark waves of a playful lake
And I have watched you grow ripe
And round like a big old chocolate cake
Fields in Mississippi did not tarnish
Your Queenly graces
And the trail to Chicago remembers
The many, many trips you have taken
Sometimes in bars I see you
Hair-curled lips-rouged mini-dress
Boots or hot hotpants
And I know you are without your King
But the magic grace of your eyes
Keeps the golden solo of your place
And I know the Dark Deep Sea will ever be . . .

The Black Woman is a poem. One cannot write about her without his muse pouring forth song. My earliest memories of life go back to the melody of life I sensed in Black women. And the last links I have with the receding past and the approaching future is Four Black Women: my wife, my two grandmothers, and my mother. Thus I cannot speak of Black Women in psychological terms, but I must sing of them because their chords are my soul and I'm their song blown against the tide of recalcitrant time.

For me, the only valid Psychology is that which flows from the reservoir of my personal experience; I must speak of Black Women as I know, and have known them. My earliest recollection of a Black Woman is my grandmother. I can remember her washing my face and tying my shoes before I had mastered those chores. Momma, as we all called her, was then about fifty-four and she was calm as an evening breeze. She ran the house, though Poppa, my grandfather, gave the orders; her voice was the only one ever raised and you better not forget to knock dust off your feet before coming into her front room. We lived on a farm a few miles outside of Clinton, Mississippi, but Momma had stopped going to the field regularly by the time my memory developed. She would oversee her garden, tend her flowers, keep house and cook, and always keep a curious eye on me so that whenever my undisciplined fingers found themselves in the sugar jar trying to get the necessary ingredients for "sweet water," I was caught in the act and my behind paid for my mischief with a hard hand or a peach tree switch. Momma was my first educator because before I could understand speech well and my steps were still unsure, she would tell me that chilluns are supposed to be seen and not heard and that little mannish boys met ill fates.

She also taught me how to keep clean, wash my face, even cleaning my ears, and brush my teeth with soda because we didn't have any toothpaste. I was also told not to break wind or fart in the presence of others and if I did then I should say "excuse me." Sometimes when Momma had to go pick blackberries or to get cool water from the springs, she would take me along with her, telling me as we went along what the names of the various trees and bushes were, telling me that if I wanted to chew gum and didn't have any money that I could scrape the bark of a sweet gum tree and come back in a few days and where I had scratched would be a wart of gum, and that I could do the same thing with pine trees and its gum was called resin.

Momma always carried a stick to fight the snakes with if we saw any; she would point out the poisonous ones to me, saying "That's a Spreading Adder and he will hiss when you get close to him," "That's a Cotton Mouth Moccasin and he opens his mouth wide and coils up," "That's a Giant Snake and when you hit it he breaks up like the weak links of a chain," "That's a Green Snake and you be careful when picking blackberries," "That's a Black Snake and he stands up on his tail and whistles and if he does, you run, because he is calling his mate to help him catch you and whip you," and "That's a King Snake, he wouldn't bite anything but other snakes and rats."

I would walk behind Momma and she would always bring along a small container for me to pick berries or carry water in. Another thing Momma did was to start us chilluns getting up with the grown folks in the morning. I got my first lessons about work, for I wasn't allowed to go back to bed or stay in the house after I got up. I had to stay out of the kitchen and out of Momma's way but be within calling distance if she needed me to bring in some stove wood, or pick up chips, or draw water, or take ice water to the field to Poppa in a pitcher if he wasn't working too far and if there were no thickets to go through.

When old folks came by the house Momma taught me the child's place by telling me to go somewhere and play, be quiet, and talk only when spoken to. I was told that unless I honored the old that my days would be cut short. I learned to say "Yes'um, Mrs." and Yah'suh, Mister" to all grown folks, white or black. I learned not to "sassy" back when Momma, Poppa, or any other grown folks told me something. Momma would tell me that I should be a "smart" little boy when I got big enough and help her and Poppa all I could. She always reminded me of the fact that the "field hands" out in the sun plowing, chopping, digging, and cutting were the stars of the family; I knew that I should get aside when they came in at twelve noon to eat. I should not pester them by getting in their way as they went about the business of washing their hands, drinking glasses of ice water, and knocking dirt out of their work shoes. I had to stand, sort of, on the sidelines of family activities and act only when invited to do so.

Momma was a kind of generational arbiter within our family for if any serious altercations emerged between members in the family, and Poppa couldn't solve it with his patriarchal power, without going side a head, then it was Momma's voice that told somebody to "put that down," "shut up" or "leave him alone" because Momma knew that nobody was going to hit her. There was a well-understood but unwritten pact among family members that if somebody dared touch Momma that he was digging his own grave, a shallow one at that. In our home, the universe of family life circled around Momma's feelings and most of the time her glow was that of a faithful sun and all we planets received adequate warmth. But sometimes traces of rheumatism would cause Momma to hobble along, or indigestion would grip her, and she would have headaches and have to lie down and rest. Somebody else would have to cook and take care of the house but things wouldn't be the same cause our worry was about Momma. Was she all right? Would she be all right tomorrow? Did she need a doctor? Even the food didn't taste the same without Momma's hands touching it. And above all, we smaller chilluns had to be very quiet and alert, careful not to disturb Momma but watchful enough to hear her calls for a "slop-jar," ice water, or help from somebody in the fields.

I remember when I got scared of something that I would grab Momma's dress tail and pull on it. I did this when a mean chicken hawk would sweep down and spear at a chicken, frightening it into uproarious calls; I did this when a setting hen would chase me pecking at me fiercely: I did this when the old gander goose would lower his head and come at me speaking in a strange dialect which let me know that he was no dove. Momma would tell me to get me a stick and to hit whatever it was that came after me and for me not to ever run away. She would then pick up a piece of a limb and shoo away whatever was bothering me.

Women in the South were primarily homemakers. They prided themselves in how well their children behaved and looked, clean and well-fed, how well they kept house and cooked, how well their flower beds and garden looked, how many jars of vegetables and fruits they put up, and how many eggs their hens laid a day. These women were the doctors and nurses of rural communities. Whenever some one got stung by wasps, yellow jackets, or bumble bees, then spider webs, vinegar, and the dirt from a dirt-darbler's nest would be mixed together as a balm. If someone's hand, foot, leg, or arm was cut, then a spider's web and soot from the chimney would be mixed to be placed in the wound to stop the flow of blood. And if one of the sisters were "down so low" that a woman was needed around the house, then one of the women from another family would go to her daily and do the house work and look after her until things got better.

Everybody called Momma "Sis Mat" or "Miss Mat." They would tell her how good she looked, how well she had raised her family, and what a good cook she was.

Religion is as much a part of the South as red clay hills, mud, and pine trees, and just about every Sunday all the grown folks would go to their different churches with the men in black suits, ties, and hats and the women in dresses, hats, and of course, purses. In fact, Religion is so much a part of the ethnos of the South that I came up believing that everybody should have a funeral and that God actually controlled everything.

Part of the role of respect that old married Black Women held came from the fact that they had brought the family through the storms of life. They had mended holes, made quilts from throw-aways, made hominy from hard corn when things were tough, made dresses and gowns from flour and meal sacks, had stayed home and stood behind their husbands when the crops were bad with bow weevils coming in and eating up everything, with the rain coming too late to help the corn crop, with not enough money left over after ginning to buy enough rations for the winter. These Black women had put up, picked up, packed up, and stored up everything that could be a meal on a cold rainy day. They had gotten cold in their joints while washing in the cold winters, had suffered near pneumonia while taking care of their chickens and small pigs. Truly, these women are Eve, the knot that binds ages, Eve of ages gone. They kept the Black Race together in America.

As I grew older I learned that all Black women are not grandmothers. My mother, aunts, and cousins were young women who went to picnics, fish fries, ball games, and honky tonks on Saturday evenings. Their lives were lively, and rich conversation flowed from them when they were together. Of course, they were all married, but they were still at that age, twenty through twenty-five, when life is defined in terms of some social activity. I can remember them talking about strange activities, dancing, drinking, and "having a ball." They did all of these things on Saturday nights and some Sunday afternoons because they had to keep house and cook on Sundays when Momma and Poppa went to church. I soon learned that Black men didn't want their wives at honky tonks having fun on Sundays when they should be at home cooking because one Sunday, my aunt was missing and my uncle had to cook dinner. After he had finished and fed us chilluns, he left and in about an hour he and his wife came back and her head had several knots on it. When we asked what happened, she said bumble bees had stung her.

I also knew that my grandfather wouldn't let the young women curse (really cuss) or talk about sex before us chilluns or in front of Momma.

Very early I knew that Black women were sought after by men, that they were prized objects because whenever violent arguments arose among my aunts and uncles, they were usually centered around—somebody else talking to his woman or him rapping to another woman. The women I knew wore pompadours, rouged their lips, and covered their faces with powders, and they didn't look like any white women I've ever seen, nor did they try to do so. I can remember my "true" mother and my aunts getting ready to go out on Saturday evenings. The preparation would begin the evening before when favorite skirts and dresses would be washed, hung out on the lines, and drenched in hot starch, then around noon on Saturday, irons would be heated on the stove and the night attire would be pressed. Before dusk invaded the brilliance of day, husbands and boyfriends would arrive and the men and women would disappear down the dusty road for a night of goodtimes before I awoke the next morning.

Later as I entered my teens and approached manhood I found Black women more beautiful, and elusive at times. My earliest criteria for Black beauty centered around how the woman was shaped and how she carried herself. In the South, the lighter skinned Black women seemed either to feel they were special or they were made to feel special.

They attracted boys like bugs are lured by bright lights on dark nights.

In Mississippi, there was always a sweet sassiness in darker sisters which made them sing: "The blacker the berry, the sweeter the juice," thus fascinating me. My first love in life was love for Black women. Segregation forced me to mature in a Black Culture where Black women held places as women. I am grateful for the fact that my understanding of Black Psychology comes from my upbringing.

You experience the economic reality of class when you realize that the only reason power, autonomy, and privileges are denied you are because of your economic status. This fact of economic class forces the Black man into a bind with respect to his woman because he cannot be sure of his future, it is taken out of his hands. He may be killed in an illegal war, he may have to work to support his fatherless family, he may not be able to go to college, or he may have to wait ten years to "get a start." This economic reality of the Black man as a poor provider is contingent upon the racist, capitalistic, and imperialistic nature of this society. And this inhuman rigidity is even harsher for the Black woman because it prevents her from having a repertoire of eligible choices as possible marital mates. The consequences of this are that very few young Black people can get married and begin contributing in an organized and relevant manner to the Black Community. Most young Black people must work very hard and search for suitable mates. But despite these handicaps, the Black woman has retained her humanness and has played a very monumental role in maintaining the Black Race.

CHAPTER FOUR

BLACK WORLDVIEW:
BLACK CHURCH
AND BLACK RITUALS

ONE INVENTS SCIENCES (AND SCIENCES are invented) like Sociology, Anthropology, Economics, Political Science, and Psychology to explain Human Behavior—and one wants to explain Human Behavior for only one reason, to predict it and by predicting it to control it. I propose that in order for one to define a relevant Black Psychology one must describe the various ways developed by the Black Man to manipulate his world, to make sense, meaning out of it. In other words, the rituals people use say more about them psychologically than any general assumptions about some kind of generic Human Nature. Black Rituals, then, are those time-proven ways passed on from one generation to the next which have enabled Black people to survive under the most trying of times. But to understand the relevance of Black Rituals, one must also understand the functions Black Religions have had in developing a Black worldview, a human worldview—a God-centered worldview.

By Black Religion I mean those ways in which Black people, in Africa and later in America, conceptualized to explain the universe and man's relationship to it and to subsequently govern man's relationship to man.

The Black man has always been a believer. His holy men, shamans, priests, preachers, musicians, poets, have always been individuals with vast spiritual powers. In the safety of Mother Africa, Black Rituals (a worldview based on spirituality) were very functional and worked very well in the communal life set-up. The priests were men who knew when to plant the crops, when to hunt the game, when to set sail upon the seas, when the rains came, what herbs were for snake bites, what herbs were for sicknesses, etc. . . . and they also knew why certain customs were obeyed and what the consequences would be if they were not obeyed. When the Europeans raped Africa, carrying off the people like buzzards do the carcasses, and inhumed them in the human hell sometimes euphemistically referred to as slavery, the Black man found himself among a people who didn't believe in anything except exploiting, destroying, dominating, indeed, the human Black man found himself amid beings who acted inhuman.

But what is crucial to any understanding of Black Rituals and their subsequent survival in the outhouse of the West is that they are ways which allow Black people to live in harmony with nature whereas European Religions— Catholicism, Protestantism, Judaism— are the obedient servants of Materialistic Thinking which means that man tries to rationally control nature, which further means, of course, that man's relationship with nature is one of conflict, disharmony.

Maybe it is because of this basic conflict or disharmonious relationship with nature that Europeans are cursed with a lack of rhythm and spontaneity. But, anyway, I maintain that Black Religion survived slavery—that is, the essentially spiritual worldview survived with man obeying the laws of nature. This does not mean that man is powerless to initiate action but just that he has a place in the universe. What I'm really driving at is that the transplanting of millions of Africans into the West was an environmental switch, but there wasn't a simultaneous cosmological or worldview adjustment—the Black man didn't adopt Materialistic Thinking as a mode of defining his world. Society in Africa was communal and nature was respected; but the West is competitive, aggressive, capitalistc, and nothing is sacrosanct. The only thing that is respected in the West is organized power—the ability to back up your position with dollars, people, and force if necessary. People who achieve in the West are doers concerned primarily with how they can manipulate the environment and other people to their best advantage, and it matters not how they do it—as long as they do it in a practical manner. The attitude which leads to success in the West is the same attitude which makes evil so profuse. There is no morality because the only criteria of good or bad is whether or not the individual succeeds.

The Black worldview was very successful at keeping the Black man's hopes and spirits alive during the cruel and barbaric times of our enslavement because there were no such things as individuals, just slaves. What emerged therefore was a communal vision where some vast spiritual power would, one day, come and snap the chains of bondage. The Spirituals, those sonic fossils of this Age of Waiting, clearly show a people out of time, lost, and anxiously depending upon some force greater than themselves to come and deliver them from their lions' den. This does not mean that the slaves didn't resist slavery but just that their dominant mode of expecting change to come about was for them to call on the Spirit of their Ancestors who were in the Spiritual world disguised as the Judaic God of the Old Testament and Christ, the Bleeding Lamb of the New Testament.

Preachers emerged as the mediators between the slaves and the God that was to deliver them. A Messiah would come to deliver them but they had to obey His messengers, the preachers.

This was a very good system during the period of slavery, and in the period immediately after slavery in which most Black people lived on farms and thus participated in an agrarian economy where the mastery of one's environment wasn't too crucial to one's success, but hard work was. The church was at the center of Black Life and did a remarkable job in creating stable conjugal families. The church gave the people the law that was to govern their daily lives. They were baptized in the church and were buried from it. When

Martin Luther King, Jr., and the members of the Southern Christian Leadership Conference decided to use the Black church as a catalyst in ending the dehumanizing system of Segregation in the South and other areas in the United States, they were acting in a manner in which the traditional Black church had acted prior to the time when most Black people became baptized.

The migration from the farm to the factory destroyed many functional relationships between the Black preachers as mediators for the Black man before some vast spiritual power who controls everything, because the ethics of urban jungles demand that individuals fight for the rewards of survival like the real animals in real jungles. This vicious system of survival necessitates that each group stick together against other groups and each group look out only for members of its own group. Also, because the city is so large the leaders of the group must try to control the factors which affect their groups. I maintain that the Black preachers were notoriously lacking in the ability to adapt their worldview from a situation where they were mediators to a situation where mediators were not needed, but where initiators were needed instead. The Black Man should have been mastering technology and the preachers should have been using the churches as the catalysts for such in Black people. But what happened is that the Black preachers continued in the roles of mediators, not before some vast spiritual power, but before organized political, economical, and cultural white power, where they voiced the aspirations of Black people. The groups whom the Black preachers were beseeching understood only organized power and were thus able to plan the kinds of social changes which destroyed the traditional power Black preachers had over their people. For example, the whole idea of social welfare destroyed the traditional role of the Black church as provider for the needy and made Black people dependent upon those who doled out relief.

The sad situation whereby Black people depend upon the wretched rulers of political parties for their essential human needs and not upon the Black church is the crux of

Black powerlessness whether it be psychological or behavioral. *The fact is that Black people are dependent upon a a church which interprets the universe and their place in it for them, but at the same time is unable to provide for them.* In other words, Black people should be more assertive, acquisitive, and active in their relationship with their environment and the preachers should be aiding them by helping them to adopt the attitudes which will allow them to conquer technology rather than keep them locked away in a belief system relevant only in communal and human societies. The weakness of Black people is the weakness of their belief in themselves to control their environment including the clouds, rivers, and the flight of objects in space.

The Black man must learn attitudes which will allow him to deal with a world that must be defined in material terms if you are to control it. I'm not advocating a material outlook on life solely, but stating that the problem Black people have is their inability to use material solutions where they are called for and spiritual solutions where they are applicable. For clearly, it doesn't matter how spiritual one is when he intends to design a machine that is going to fly, for he must define the sky in operational, measurable terms. He must try to control both the weight and speed of the object that will fly, which means that he must master the material aspects of flying.

The cities transformed Black preachers into deliverers of Black votes, beggars for Black humanity, bargainers with everybody except Black people. The social changes the Black church participated in, in urban areas, were for the most part changes dealing with short-range programs: getting people hired, getting people on relief, etc., but never any long-range programs designed to bring about any fundamental social changes. To engage in such long-range programs, I warn you, demands that one understand the structure of the society one lives in, that one understands how changes come about in this society, and that one believes that he can through his own efforts bring this about. One must be an initiator to bring about change.

The Black preachers were always reactors—they reacted to bad situations before Black people made them worse or better by taking them into their own hands.

Even the Civil Rights Movement began as a student protest movement and the preachers came along and interpreted the significance of it and then proceeded to devise an ideology and tactic that white folks would accept. The importance of the church's role in the Civil Rights Movement is that it participated in a program designed to bring about social change, end segregation and discrimination.

This was a return to the spirit of the late 1900's when the church was an initiator of social change with leaders like Bishop Turner. The weakness of the church's participation in the Civil Rights Movement was that its participation was designed largely to restrain Black people. There were no two-way dialogue with Black people where their insights were considered and incorporated. It seemed as if the church felt it had to hold back Black Sensibility or otherwise this unruly sensibility would wreck the golden opportunity to reach the Promised Land of American Equality.

CHAPTER FIVE

BLACK RELIGION,
BLACK CULTURE,
AND AMERICAN IDEOLOGY

THE BLACK POWER MOVEMENT HAS been the most misunderstood phenomenon yet, especially by Black Leaders. First of all, Black people have always had a distinctive lifestyle that automatically made them different from other ethnic groups. But the significance of the Black Power Movement has been that Black people are now deciding that they will define what is valuable in Black Life. This is a very radical, even revolutionary manuever and has the explosive nature of a sensitivity session, a national sensitivity session. For what's involved at bottom is a readjustment of the self-image of all people in this country.

If Black people are to define what a proper self-image is for themselves, then it means that whatever other people think of them is invalid. It also means that those ways of viewing the world sanctioned by the dominant institutions, both white and black, must be challenged. What this does is to threaten the very basis of power for all Black leaders. This is particularly threatening to Black preachers because their traditional roles have been those of telling Black people who they are, what their problems are, and what must be done to solve them. Also, the Black preachers' roles as interpreters of reality for Black people have necessarily caused them to make compromises with the White Power Structure—compromises which meant, in effect, that the

Black preachers, and only the Black preachers, are the direction-givers for Black people.

Thus when the Black Power Movement opted to utilize a concept of Black Cultural Nationalism as an ideological framework which would restore the Black man's dignity by laying the rudiments of a Black Nation, the Black preachers found themselves without a role in the Black community after nearly two centuries of unchallenged rule. Thus everywhere Black preachers could be seen buying tikis, getting naturals, modeling dashikis, learning new handshakes, and African syllables. But to understand the complex nature of the problem one must take into account the fact that while the Black preachers lacked ideology, they still had a programmatic outlet for their philosophies—the Black church; and the Black Cultural Nationalists were without any program, but had an ideology that was Black. What the Black preachers did in this crisis was to accuse the Black Cultural Nationalists of being anti-religious, racist, and radical.

The conflict between the Black preachers and the Black Cultural Nationalists heightened as Black Artists began erecting a picture of reality which turned the eyes of Black people forward to Africa, rather than backwards to Europe. And it was this anchoring of all Black Philosophy in Africa that created a wide cleavage between Black artists and Black preachers whose minds were afloat on boards heading towards Europe, and the artists circled above the people without a suitable place to land. Part of the problem for both Black preachers and Black artists is to join the ideology of the Black Cultural Nationalists to the programmatic structure of the Black church.

Such a move will destroy the competitive struggle between the Black preacher and the Black artist for the role of interpreter-of-reality-for-Black-people. This would revolutionize the Black church by making it address itself to the serious problems of modernizing its philosophy to meet the needs of a people enslaved in urban jungles in an industrial society where the individual must be taught to manipulate his environment. If the Black church can successfully inject Black Cultural Nationalism into its theological framework, then the spiritual needs of Black people can be met and a violent struggle within the Black community for leadership will not occur. Black artists can work within a Black church that's flexible enough to allow individuals the use of their own phenomenological insights to give directions/create positive images/pave paths to our ancestral home.

Resolution of the conflict the Black church has with a modern technological society must come through a reconciliation with Black Cultural Nationalism. Black Cultural Nationalism is doing for Black people, today, what the Black church did for them during and immediately following slavery—creating a belief system that's healthy for the spirit of Black people and functional enough to provide for their physical needs. What such a reconciliation will do is to relieve the Black church of the necessity of becoming theological schizophrenics (like white churches) where on the one hand an entirely materialistic explanation of all reality is given, and simultaneously, on the other hand, the Lamb of God still has the hallowed-Creator-Saviour place in the scheme of things. A reconciliation means that an analysis of the structure of society must replace the Bible in terms of what is a guide for action. It means that Black preachers must replace prayers with social planning; it means that Black Theology must view its interpretation of God through the lens of a correct appraisal of African History, and of the role holy men play in all African societies.

Black artists must submit to those institutions working directly in the process of Black Nation Building. If the Black church changes into such an institution, then Black artists must work within the church.

The Black man is a doer, not a planner. He acts now, not later. He explodes spontaneously and does not wait like a time bomb. This mode of coping with life makes the Black man particularly prone to acting out his hostility, either against himself (suicide) or against others (homicide). A very startling finding in *Black Suicide* by Herman Hendin is the fact that most Blacks who commit suicide and homicides are between the ages of twenty and thirty-five. This is very interesting because the ratio of suicide whites to suicide blacks is eleven to four, but the ratio within the age brackets of twenty to thirty-five is two to one for blacks, especially urban Blacks. *What is very meaningful about these statistics is the fact that Black Rituals are not equipping young urban Blacks with the tools necessary for them to successfully cope with their oppressive situation.* And this is alarming because it means that young Blacks are acting, or seem to be acting, as if they must individually strike out as their impulses dictate.

Their approaches to the problems are not systematic, cohesive, and rigorously pursued. Their actions seem to say that "We can't come up with any solutions but we will show them how we feel about things." But notice that their attack is always directed toward some individual, and not against systems. I believe that a plausible reason a young urban Black is prone to act violently against himself or against others is because he has been oriented into a society where the dominant worldview is that man does not have control over his environment. For what impulsive actions mean in the final analysis is that the individual is helpless to do anything about his situation and the only way for him to get any kind of attention and/or gratification is to spontaneously explode without any preconceived plans, and any alternate plans. This can be traced back to the Black Rituals' insistence that God alone rules the universe and that man is a child and must obey nature. The preacher is God's mundane bargainer and the Bible the reference book for all cures. The Black man is never told that he can, through knowldge, control his environment. There is always some concept of a place for the Black man. He must take his problems to others (God or leaders) to have them solved for him.

My theory is that Black Religion adequately equips a child with a vision suitable for a child's world, but that as an individual grows to adulthood, that the rituals of childhood are not sufficient to provide the answers to the problems raised by facing life in a chaotic, urban, industrial society where the actions and decisions of men definitely decide the fate of millions (that is men who have economic and political power make rules which are causes to what happens to men who don't have power). In fact, at the base of any Industrial Society is the materialistic belief that man can control his environment to such an extent that production can be predicted. Thus any man not trained to believe that he can manipulate his environment to meet his needs is lost in an industrial society because the only key to power is for individuals with common aims to join in organizations, parties, unions, etc. . . . and develop the skills, acquire the capital and commission somebody to carry out their plan agreed upon by the group. This means that organizations in industrial societies replace functions of institutions found in communal societies. But the Black individual acts as if he is still in a communal society where all people believe in God and all men have the human concerns of society as whole foremost in their minds—particularly, those men who make and enforce the laws. This belief causes the Black man to become frustrated and blame individuals for their shortcomings in this world: it causes Black men to see only the symptoms, not the causes, for the structure of the American society prevents most people from living human existence and if one wishes to change the quality of life for individuals then one must make structural changes in this society.

The Black individual who reaches adulthood without having had the benefit of technological training is totally unprepared to control his life. For what technology does for the individual is to provide him with the skills necessary for achievement in our society. This peculiar technological dependency is a by-product of the fact that environments in industrialized societies are no longer natural. They cannot automatically give you what life needs because the rise of technology has seen men intercede in the natural processes and gain a wretched kind of exploitative control over them. In fact, a dominant theme in American History over the last hundred years has been man's continual quest to control his environment. All of the various Land-Grant Colleges were founded to train individuals in knowledge and skills sufficient to manipulate key factors in the environment and thereby make the resources more exploitable. But young Black individuals lack such training and when they reach the portals of adulthood, they face a grave crisis because they cannot go back and cope as a child and neither are they equipped to cross the bridge and engage in the fierce competitiveness for status and a suitable image of themselves as men.

The fact that most suicides and homocides Black men commit are committed between the ages of twenty and thirty-five indicates that after thirty-five the Black individual ceases to struggle against his environment and accepts a fate for himself in it, thus returning to the philosophical attitudes taught him in Black churches when he was very young: resignation in what was pre-ordained by the Lord's Will. Since most white individuals commit suicide after forty-five indicates that their intense indoctrination in the practices and philosophy of technology prepares them well for roles as young men when status and security (economic, material) dictate a healthy self-image, but after forty-five, the whole question of the meaning of life is raised and the whites seem ill-prepared to utilize any spiritual concepts to make their world clear enough for survival.

Let's face it! The Black church is the only institution in existence that is capable of reversing a trend of thinking that has brought Black people to the very banks of annihilation. First, the Black preachers are the historical leaders of most Black people and their words in the churches will be heard by more people than belong to any other organizations; second, most Black people are victims of beliefs which have their origin in the Black church whether they go to church or not, or whether they have ever been there; third, a change of religion will not eliminate the crisis most Black people face because most Black people are going to die Christians.

Thus, the problem becomes one of how the Black church can be utilized to strengthen the weak survival structure of Black life. I see the most revolutionary potential in the Black church as being its capacity to institutionalize a worldview that unites Blacks in this country with Blacks everywhere, and prepares Black urban youth in the skills so badly needed to keep body and soul married until the age of thirty-five. But the program I envision is a comprehensive one whereby Black churches will organize into some operational structure in which the financial resources can be pooled.

The churches must sponsor an alternative educational system similar to that of the Catholic church—the reason being that since Black people are not presently organized to make the existing educational system (the public one) work for them, they must immediately begin to prepare a system which will end the destruction of whole generations of Black minds. This means that Black preachers must be trained in areas which allow technology to grow: mathematics, biology, chemistry, economics, electronics, engineering, and physics. Religious ethics can still be taught, but Black children must be taught that they can control their environment, living space, that they can discover nature's laws which govern life (discover the laws, not change them).

Change won't come about easy for the Black churches because of the peculiar circumstances under which the Black church has developed. There now exist a number of separate churches which are psychological tribes, each with their own autonomy. It seems that the diverse and uncooperative nature of the churches makes them more of a tribal problem for Black Africans in America than there are for the different tribes in the Motherland. However, if prominent Black preachers began teaching about a new mission (building schools, hospitals, cultural centers, etc.), it would spread like poisonous gas.

This move on the part of the churches will, however, alienate them from the white Liberals because Black people will be determining *what* is needed to be done and how it is to be done—which means that Ford, Rockefeller, etc. . . . can keep their grants and their scholars who always find what they are sent out to find. I mean that Black preachers have to demand that they be the real interpreters of Black life rather than experts trained in the specious rhetoric of deception.

If Black churches are unable to establish alternative educational systems and to be a leadership force independent of the mainstream, then the Black church no longer has a function in Black life. For at this point, Black people must seek *other* ways, structures, ideologies and strategies to solve their problems. If the present Black church cannot make a commitment to Black liberation, then why must Black people continue to attend them? For what can an institution do if it does not insure the survival of its members?

A case in point is the issue of establishing a Third Party where a chief spokesman is a Black minister who is constantly on T.V., in magazines, in newspapers, and speaking before different political groups, drumming up support for a Third Party to challenge the two dominant ones in the 1972 elections. But one must ask why doesn't this brilliant young politician try to organize the Black churches as a political party—if he did, then he would have a Third Party.

I sometimes wonder just who the Black preachers are leading, because they try to ally themselves with Indians, poor whites, Chicanos—other oppressed people—when they have not organized their own Black oppressed constituency of thirty-five million. Do they believe that Black people can be an effective political party? If so, then why don't they just organize Black people to oppose anyone not picked by them? If Black people cannot be an effective political party, then why pretend to lead a people who are incapable of being organized around what the preachers advocate?

A good understanding of Black History reveals that the threat to Black survival has increased proportionally to the degree that the Black Man has become urbanized. Their reason here is that *urban societies are controlled by the dominant interests of definable groups who are in possession of power. They* determine where you stay, how much rent you pay, the number and quality of schools for your children, the kinds of jobs available, and who will man them.

The deadly aspect of this kind of system is that though educational opportunities are unfair, they (the rulers) still use education as a main criteria for allowing individuals to participate in the wider economic and social circles. This cycle always finds the Black man outside of a circle unbroken.

The Black church can break this circle by providing alternatives and welding its members into *one* political body. It is the most expedient way for Black Power to begin to wear the garments of operationalism. Black people can't simply return to Mother Africa this instant and in order to survive here in America, one must thoroughly understand the system and develop pockets of power where some degree of independent manueverability is maintained. Black preachers can be catalysts and Black people can become the force that will turn the tides of America.

CHAPTER SIX

THE "F" RITUALS;
THE WAY
WE BLACK FOLK DO IT

FREEDOM DANCER

I have never seen my fathers as old men
Always they are long gone before
I learn to walk straight
Their lives are legends
Black Women tell me of . . .
I'm a stranger to myself
And must have legends to cloak me
And I set out over dreams searching
Searching for visions my fathers held . . .
There is a threatening cloud overhead
A perilous storm waits in my path
Thunder roars and lightning laughs
But I wander through spiritual trails
And explode into happy downpours
Of mandrops—found in sweet songs
I flow down years of slavery
Overflowing into flames of war
I'm a freedom dancer
The African dreams of Black Men
Lead me on through soft rhythms . . .
I hear the beacon of pain
Slipping his fangs into Black Backs
I hear the sourness of Starvation

Causing Black Children's tummies to expand
And oh I hear the silence of Black Manacts
I hear the silence . . . the silence . . .
The silence of Black Men
And my feet drip in martial halos
I'm a freedom dancer
These holy steps I take
Are musical shadows of visions
My fathers held . . .
I flow down the years like rivers
And my movements are African Seasons
I'm rich as a coconut
Mighty as the kiss of falling dew
And I downpour in African mandrops. . . .

When it comes to rituals, we Black people describe our world in hedonic terms "I like this" or "I don't like this," while the white man describes his world in terms of pragmatism, "I think this is best because it will allow me to achieve" or "I don't think this is best because it will not allow me to reach my goals." We Black people have perfected sixteen rituals which begin with "F" that we can always fall back on to get us out of a crisis. We have a Ritual of *Faith* whereby we say to the world "I believe." We are not skeptics, distrustful of everything. We commit all our actions to a belief in God, in preachers, in leaders, in ads, and in everything except ourselves. This Ritual of Faith runs counter to scientific thinking which is the cornerstone of technology because science rests upon a certain amount of skepticism. Skepticism and science are related because with the establishment of science reliable methods for measuring phenomena were developed and what occurs when you measure or experiment is that there are always so many factors to control that there are always slight errors to be accounted for, which means that the probability of an occurrence is never guaranteed on the first trial.

This probalistic thinking means, in effect, that the individual is skeptical because he knows that he has not controlled all the factors. But his view forces him to constantly seek better methods to make his predictions more probable. People who have faith admit that there is someone or something higher than they who/which has the power to do things that they cannot do. This is nonsense, in so far as power is concerned, because history shows through the rise of technology in the West, that man has unlimited potential for controlling his environment, for better or for worse. Belief in God should give man a purpose in life and not rid man of a strong belief in himself as lord of the physical universe. We Black people in America must learn from a very early age that the world is nothing but a big toy which we can manipulate.

In the sexual arena, we Black people be very aggressive; our language is action-oriented for we "lay pipe," "bust nuts," "tear up asses," "slaughter on killing floors" or just "grind." In the Ritual of Fucking we Black people say "I will show you that I am a man." The important thing here is that we use our bodies spontaneously, improvisationally, according to our current feelings and we achieve our goals without planning far in advance. I'm not saying that we can't plan, simply that we don't. The attitudes whereby we say "I know I'm a man and can prove it so long as I don't need to learn anything from books" is the wellspring of Black creativity, Soul—Black genius. For it means that we Black people have never learned to suppress our affectivity when coping with our environment. In other words, we Black people don't conceptualize fucking and then study how to do it. We simply rely on our sense of rhythm to carry the day for us.

Sex can be related to poetry, music, dancing and singing with us Black people, in that we need no models to imitate in order to achieve. It is in this sense, this feeling of absolute competence in handling anything concerning our bodies, that makes us Black people so creative, so human. We have not been trained to deliberately wear a mask in order to deceive others and thus gain our ends. But our spontaneous, open, and free responses to life cripple us when dealing with European manipulations.

The Europeans train their children from the first day of life to be very selective, very careful, to give the response accepted by the majority. In fact, they train their children that emotionality harms the ability to reason, thus they become unfeeling like machines and perform acts according to some social blueprint ingrained in them by the socializing agencies of their culture. I have always felt that white folks didn't laugh unless a sign was held up saying "laugh." Their actions don't emanate from feelings deep within them but from what they feel is an appropriate response for them, for any particular group, at any particular time. The fact is that Europeans are not individuals but are patterned carbon copies of the developmental theories of their social architects. They can function without visible leaders or interpreters, because they have been programmed like a computer to do what the programmer expects of them. But we Black people have not been programmed to do anything. We are taught to restrain our actions whether positive or destructive and let others do our acting for us.

Society controls us by taking the initiative out of our hands, but simultaneously blames us for not having any initiative. We Black people accept or believe what others can do for us because our most powerful institution, the church, has conditioned us to be children with respect to our environment. It teaches us that certain things are off limits at both the speculative and behavioral levels. This keeps us with a central faith in humanity, which is all right in a human society. But it is very destructive for us in the American situation, where the dominant institutions try to and do control its members by assigning them functions like a designer does to nuts and bolts in a machine, and by either forcing the individuals to serve the functions assigned to them or destroying them and replacing them with other nuts and bolts that will.

The controllers of the American system are very much aware of what they are doing. That is why advertising is so big and successful. It is founded on the premise that "we can program man to do what we want him to do without his ever knowing it; further those who we can't program are insignificant enough to be ignored and called stupid, or represent a threat and must be systematically annihilated."

Closely related to the Ritual of Faith is the Ritual of Fate. In it we Black people say "I accept your decision, environment. We cannot do anything to alter you. You are beyond our comprehension. We submit."

Two very similar phenomena, the Black Panthers and the Black Street Gangs, appear on the surface to be taking their fate into their own hands but a close scrutiny of their activities reveals that they are really hollering for help. And a very interesting fact to keep in mind is that most of them (Panthers and Gang members) are between the ages of twenty and thirty-five, precisely the ages in which most Black people commit suicide and homicide.

The super relevancy of this correlation must not be overlooked because one suspects that the individuals involved are only reacting to immediate impulses rather than doing something they know will work. This is dangerous, because at a time when planning is so vital, when the author of an action is to bring that action to fruitition, our actors are without plans. And the real disgusting thing about the situation is that those leaders who are most vociferous intimate that Black Panthers and the Black Youth Gangs are going to do something about their problems.

Such rhetoric could be mistaken to mean that the Black Panthers and Black Youth Gangs have some systematic, programatic, plausible plan that can be used to bring about change. But what emerges upon close inspection is simply groups of anxious individuals whose visions have been soaked in the deep wells of Black religion, and who thus have no concept of how they can defeat the system. They are simply baffled and impulsively acting to wreak violence on others, Blacks mainly (homocide) or against themselves (suicide). Young Blacks who are members of either group come to the same conclusion individually. Thus what you have in both the Black Panthers and Black Youth Gangs is the generalization of individual pathology to an impulsive ideology for group survival.

There is also the Ritual of Fear whereby we Black people say "I stand before you almighty environment, helplessly." The attitude we develop about God is the same attitude we adopt concerning our environment. A good analogy is the two murders of Robert Kennedy and Martin Luther King, Jr. When the New York Senator was felled by hot lead, his first words to his would-be rescuers, as the press reported, was for them to get away from around him so he could breathe freely. What he did was to resort to what knowledge he had of how the human body works and tried to save his own life with it. His response was a practical one. On the other hand, when the Moses of Montgomery felt the intrusion of deadly lead, he cried out, again as reported in the reliable press, "Oh God, have mercy." He was helpless; he trembled before the powerful forces working against him, and his attitude was one of helplessness.

This is important because it means that we Black people view death as God-controlled while our white counterparts view death as just another environmental factor that can be controlled by them.

We Black people also have the Ritual of Fussing, whereby we literally say "I'm right, you can't change me." This attitude is related to our vulnerability to believing we must believe in the whole hog, not just one or two inferential ribs. Also, by believing, we accept one alternative as the only alternative; everybody is wrong.

This mode of thinking prevents us from unifying, creates among us little credo pockets, clogs up the stream of pragmatism. For it means that "if I'm a revolutionary who shoots at the pigs, then for everybody else to be a revolutionary he must shoot at pigs also and if he does not, then he is counter-revolutionary." Or it means "that only Christ is the Saviour, or only Allah, or only Malcolm X was the true prophet, or Black preachers are God's sole interpreters." This tendency on our part as a people to see, particular alternative as eternal moral truths runs counter to our European counterparts who see everything in relative, pragmatic, functional terms.

In technological societies, one must do that which is practical at the time. He cannot be concerned about always using the same technique to solve different problems; one must always seek a better alternative.

Then there is the pathetic Ritual of Fighting, whereby we Black people say "I can win." Again, our actions don't grow out of any plan but erupt from the volcano of our grumbling impulses. Usually, a fight occurs when someone hurts or breaks our spontaneous coping style by insulting us, putting us down, stepping on our alligator shoes, or outdoing us. In most cases, these altercations occur with our very close friends and relatives. The fights are very rarely planned by the combatants; they just occur. Again when we look at our European counterparts we see them controlling their impulses and emitting a learned response in hostile situations. It does not mean that the embarrassing or insulting incident isn't over, only that whatever one does is planned, that interpersonal relations have been reduced to a mechanism. He will get even when he gets the upper hand.

These styles of coping/dealing are important in an industrial, urban, technological maze; the offended cannot personally strike out at that which offends him but must organize to gain power, then move to redress the wrong. In other words, white folks make laws that protect them only and reject laws which protect others if it is not to their economic interest, while we Black people either want to obey all laws or disregard all laws. As a group, we haven't reached the point where we deliberately organize to make laws for ourselves, that is, at the community level. A unified, relevant Black church can eliminate the Ritual of Fighting by providing the mechanism for us Black people to move politically to insure our command over our own destiny.

This will be a dangerous step by the churches—as dangerous as the strides made by ante-bellum preachers against the vicious fangs of slavery. It means that the Black church will be the only place the Black preacher will be welcomed to speak and it means that he must live among his flock.

The Ritual of Favorites is a very devious ritual because behind the bold persona of "I'm blessed" there lurks the limped reality of "I'm picked by the almighty environment" meaning "I'm not really responsible for my success." Traces of this kind of thinking are visible in the ways we Black people dig what our artists are saying. "God Bless the Child That Got Its Own," the suggestion being if he does not have it then he cannot get it. The same remark jumps up when brothers are rapping about Gale Sayers or O. J. Simpson and you hear "moves like what they got can't be learned" or "I wish I was as tall as Lew Alcindor is" or "Some people got it like Martin Luther King" or "James Brown is a natural dancer."

The first cousin of the Ritual of Favorites is the Ritual of Fortune which says "I was lucky" and which means "that it's all in the cards which the environment is dealing and if you get a bad hand that's the way it is. The dealer should never be questioned. He is the dealer and you shouldn't try to influence what he deals you. Just wait awhile, you may get lucky."

The Ritual of Fortune is very pronounced among poor Black people where we play numbers for ages trying to catch a hit. But it is very difficult to get us to organize our precincts to become independent and control the ward and all the political booty. To take such a step would mean that we would have to actively challenge the political environment rather than waiting to get lucky. Everything in Black life is psychologized in theological terms.

The Ritual of Friends says "We are alike," and means "that the environment made us alike. It was the carving hand of fate that earmarked us for our position and we must not leave our orbit." Color per se is not a determiner in the Ritual of Friends. Friends are people who are made for one another. Again the implication is that if they are not made for one another then they cannot be for one another. In other words, people can't voluntarily change to adjust to the ways of other people. I feel that this attitude develops because our Black child-rearing institution is not spelled out. Everything that's done is sort of done in reaction to some vague but insistent instinctual need. The Black church must master the information dealing with Developmental Psychology, reconcile it with the theological creed, then manualize it for us Black people. There are acres of evidence which conclusively demonstrate that the way babies are programmed from the cradle predictably determines their potentialities until the grave.

What whites like Dr. Spock, Sigmund Freud, Alfred Adler, Carl Jung, Viktor Frankyl, Karen Horney, Harry Stack Sullivan, Karl Marx, William James, John Dewey, Charles Darwin, Albert Einstein, Carl Rogers, Jean Piaget, Alfred Binet, and David Wechsler have done for whites, Black preachers must begin to do for Black families.

The Ritual of Friends' brother is the Ritual of Foes which says "They are different, therefore they are my enemies" which means "that they act differently and therefore they cannot act like me and I cannot act like them." The Ritual of Friends and the Ritual of Foes are responsible for the many, many cliques found among us Black folks. One of the reasons the Black Power Movement took such a bombastic rhetorical turn after Stokley Carmichael injected the phrase "Black Power" into the already live body of Civil Rights jargon is that people who talked alike and dressed alike were "friends" and those who talked softer and wore more conventional garments were "foes" and vice versa.

We Black people have a Ritual of Faking which says "At least, I can pretend; and besides, who will know me from the real thing?" This is most evident in our concern with wearing the latest, drinking the latest, driving the latest, and living in the latest. We wear the appearance of financial success without having the steel skeleton of it. When we come from parties we talk for days about how good so-and-so looked, or about how good such-and-such tasted, or how smooth the ride was in this-and-that car, and how much money we spent having a ball. We hardly ever talk about how much security we have, or how much property our organization is buying to build hospitals, schools, markets. We don't even talk about how we have put away dollars for our children's future.

The Ritual of Fun complements the Ritual of Faking by saying "I'm living it up this minute, because I don't know whether I can live it up the next minute or not. I don't have any control over the next second." All the night clubs, honky-tonks, churches, and dance halls reinforce the Ritual of Fun because they are places where emotional outlets can overflow now, this minute. Fun cannot be misinterpreted for happiness because happiness is buttressed by an assurance of something and fun is a flight toward doing now what tomorrow may not allow me to do.

The Ritual of Funerals is the crowning achievement of our passivity toward our environment. We Black people ask the question of "When I go, how will it be?" in the Ritual of Funerals. At funerals we make ado over how alive the corpse looks, how well shaved it is, how many people attend, and how good the casket looks. The meaning of all this seems that We Black people hope to make our funerals more successful than our lives. We are helpless to master this environment, but we are concerned about ourselves after death. There is real anguish at Black funerals. The survivors weep because they are helpless to do anything for the deceased but there is beneath their suffering a queer kind of happiness that, after all, the Almighty's Will has been done. Death, then, for us Black people is beyond our control but we are concerned about our final appearance before returning to the elements.

The Ritual of the Future prepares us Black people for the Ritual of Funerals by telling us "maybe tomorrow, but not now." We Black people always put off for tomorrow for somebody else to do what we can do today. A classic example is the way every generation talks about "how the young people ain't gon take no stuff of' the white man. They gon bring about a change." This kind of psychological bullshit relieves the present generation of doing anything by psychologizing. To bring about a change tomorrow in a social sense, one must actively shape certain things now, but we Black people wait. And this may be the rationale behind CP time: "ain't no need of me rushing NOW cause ain't nothing gon happen" meaning "I ain't never done anything and I ain't about to start now."

Sneaking up on the heels of the Ritual of Future is the Ritual of First whereby we Black people merely wait cause "when the time comes I gon get what I deserve. 'Look at Bill Cosby, he waited and see where it got him, and Flip Wilson and Sidney Poitier, and Senator Brooke, but look what happened when you try to do too much like Stokely Carmichael, and Malcolm X, and Fred Hampton, and Rap Brown, and Martin Luther King; naw, I ain't gon try too hard, I'm gon just wait.' "

Lastly, the primary ritual is the Ritual of Fathers which says to us Black people "only one among you at a time can have a will, and need to use it." The whole idea of making a personality the embodiment of theistic ideals is a reflection of this "man, Malcolm is a Black God," but why not every Black man a Black God. We Black people must place our leaders above ourselves in terms of human possibility.

"The poets will weigh you down with wisdom," but why can't Black men weigh one another down with the truth about ourselves. I feel that this is what the Black Culture Movement threatened to do to make all Black people equal —but before this endeavor could be institutionalized there emerged among us maulanas, imamus, prophets, princesses, etc.—certain Black people began placing other individuals above the herd. This is dangerous because in effect, it is saying that only certain people are capable of doing what needs to be done; bullshit! I feel this is the only way Black leaders know how to deal with their Black constituency— treating them as children, often foster children. This psychological oligarchism is detrimental to our sense of feeling the power of our own body and mind. It must be destroyed. The Black church can institute programs, perhaps sensitivity groups, to restore the integrity to all Black individuals but simultaneously making us an integral part of the large Black body politic.

Related to the whole notion of rituals is we Black people's belief in a psychological reckoning. You develop into what you become but you accept or refuse opportunities when they come—"my boy got a good mother wit 'bout cars and ain't no need paying all that money for him to go to some kind of school where they takes cars apart." "Everybody got a certain mother wit for something and I can't see why these young folks talking about what they want to be. Maybe it ain't for them." Needless to say, our European counterparts have developed tests to tap behavior in such a way that their educators can tell at a very early age what their children should be able to do and what they should do. White children don't have mother wit, they have aptitudes which are influenced by the kinds of toys they play with, the museums they visit, the T.V. programs they watch, and the special training their parents provide for them.

You don't just sing if you have a good voice or play an instrument if you have a good ear. You are given music lessons from year-two through year-twenty and the consequences are that you become a very accomplished musician.

58

I'm not saying that we Black people's mode of thinking and doing is wrong, just that it is impractical if we are to control our destiny in America's urban, industrial, and technological pig sty. In order to survive, the inhabitants of industrial societies must control their political, social, economic environment. The reason animals become extinct is because they cannot control the changes taking place in their habitat and thus when conditions become unlivable, they perish. The same will be true of us Black people in America unless we begin to decide that which will influence our environment. This means the medical facilities, educational facilities, housing facilities, law-enforcing agencies, law-making agencies, judicial agencies, economic agencies, political agencies, and cultural agencies.

Our task will not be an easy one because white institutions will not train us to defeat the power they have over us. We must do this ourselves and we must use our strongest institution as a base. The Black church must become more relevant or, like the Buffalo a century ago, we Black people will perish, but this time in urban prairies.

CHAPTER SEVEN

THE CRISIS NOW; HOW THE TECHNOLOGICAL SYSTEM WORKS

RECENTLY WHEN THE REVOLUTIONARY-black-cultural-nationalism rhetoric was at its highest pitch, I had the misfortune of hearing a very, very famous Black Power advocate say "Africa don't need no sociologists, psychologists, and anthropologists; she needs plumbers, farmers, ditch-diggers, mechanics, etc. . . ." I took the remarks of the young man, who incidentally was on T.V., conditioning his Black brothers with his rap, to mean that sociology, psychology, and anthropology had no role to play in a liberation movement. But a careful analysis of his rap revealed that he was completely ignorant of why and how technological societies operate. First of all, sociologists, psychologists, and anthropologists are specialists who have developed techniques for assessing human behavior and they are found only in the most advanced (technologically speaking) societies measuring behavior so that predictions and correct planning can be made. Every advanced society has made specialists of psychology, sociology, and anthropology, because in order to implement change in an orderly way, one must have reliable indicators which predict what will happen. It has been shown, for instance, that children who score very high on the I.Q. (really Standford-Binet and Wechsler Intelligence) tests have the potential for developing and fulfilling very crucial jobs (roles) in the society, thus these individuals are selected out and given special education for those roles (scientists, doctors, lawyers, writers, ministers, etc. . . .).

The important thing here is that it is very efficient to allow only those who have known potential for succeeding and achieving the opportunity to do so. But this is true of all societies; for instance, every child in non-industrial societies doesn't have the same chance of becoming a chief, a medicine man, or sculptor. There is some basis for selecting out who will fulfill which roles. The greatest impetus to the rise of technology in Europe was the ascendancy of materialistc thinking, positivism, the right of reason over authority, mysticism and religion. This great event occurred by the middle of the 19th Century and was culminated with Darwin's theory of evolution. For if man evolved from a lower form of animal then, perhaps, the key to understanding man's behavior lies in an unbiased understanding of animal behavior. This meant that man was not free, there was no soul, there is no right and wrong, because man learns everything from his experience.

Pavlov sealed the deal for materialism with his classical conditioning experiments which showed that if the correct stimuli were presented, then the behavior (response) of the animal or individual could be predicted without the organism having anything to do with it. Also, at the same time that Pavlov was demonstrating how behavior could be controlled, psychometricians were busy devising techniques for evaluating individual differences.

All Black people can't be plumbers, all can't be bricklayers, all can't be lawyers, all can't be doctors, all can't be teachers, but the question is how do you choose the individuals for the different roles if you don't have specialists to do the choosing.

I feel that since only capitalistic countries have developed sophisticated (exceptions, Russia and China) methods for handling human behavior that certain advocates of Socialism believe that knowledge of psychology, sociology, and anthropology will automatically bring in private property. It's not true of Russia—where Pavlov's ideas are as valuable as Lenin's in allowing Russia to industrialize.

The problem of Black people all over the world is that their intellectuals have never had real power within their own Black communities because they have been a threat to the preacher elite who knows what the Truth is. In Africa, the dominant worldview will not let an architect of human behavior come along and destroy myths centuries old.

In Europe, the names of materialists like Charles Darwin, Sigmund Freud, Karl Marx, Albert Einstein, and Alfred Binet have come to be synonymous with knowledge, and the man of the cloth has had to adjust his ideas about deities to accommodate the axioms of the materialists. And the universities of Europe were responsible for producing the brains who "spread civilization" to the rest of the world and this could not be done with the knowledge of biblical texts solely. There had to be transportation facilities, mapping techniques, and the belief that man could do anything if he tried.

What shocked me about the Black Nationalist Movement is that instead of emphasizing the technical aspects of life (automation, urbanization, industrialization) that it preferred to rap about ancient African gods as if they would come and free Black people. The gods didn't stop the white boy and gun powder when they brought our forefathers over here, and they won't stop him if he decides to pacify us permanently. What we need to know is how can we do things, techniques, ways of doing, not ways of believing.

There is nothing beautiful about man and his use of power whether it be in an industrial, capitalistic society or a communal, rural society. The fact is, that those few individuals in power make decisions. All Black people don't make decisions anywhere in the world—only the political leaders do (so why must the masses be made to respect leaders who are incapable of delivering them from oppression?). And this is the case as long as the goal of Black nations is industrialization (automatizing their economy); and if industrialization is the goal, then how do the individuals know whether the newer technocracies will be any better than the older ones. Now that Russia is a world power and production and GNP are more important than the people, the revolutionary writers are being jailed. Socialism in a large, urban, technological society is no better for the individuals than capitalism in the same societies because in all cases the needs of the individuals are controlled by somebody else.

Technology ain't got nothin' to do with ideology whether it be "socialism," "capitalism" or "pan-africanism" because technology deals with the individuals' ability to control his environment. It is an approach to life which demands that one learns the most pragmatic way of doing things. I think ideologies are the motivators of individuals in societies. Why do people build rockets, who can afford a heart transplant, and who will own the SST which will be built with everybody's money? The fact is that there are no non-European countries that have been industrialized and controlled by their own native people for fifty consecutive years. There is Japan, but when the West saw that technology did in three decades what the Japanese gods had not done in twenty centuries, they conspired and whipped her back into her place. China shows signs of becoming a major industrial power, but will the "human values" persevere through the transformation?

Black Liberation is a movement of a people who haven't mastered either the philosophy or techniques (methods) of technology, against a people whose religion is technology. Black people must become pragmatic in dealing with their problems. We must correctly assess what needs to be done if liberation is to be a reality; then we must decide how to do it. Also, we must prepare to make the necessary adjustments when experience shows that certain steps are unnecessary or cumbersome. Mastery of technology will aid Black Liberation all over the world because it tells the individual The How, and the only questions left are: The What and The When. Sociologists, psychologists, anthropologists, dedicated, and working in the interest of Black people and not in the interest of suave black academic journals and academicians can greatly accelerate the process of Black people becoming more technological. For at the base of technology is specialization and specialization can only be a pragmatic reality if the individual's capacities are measurable—this means testing, and grouping and teaching individuals according to their aptitudes.

This is work that both psychologists and sociologists are familiar with. If urban, industrial complexes are envisioned, then structural changes will take place in society and thus the anthropologists can lend valuable analysis and planning.

The whole Black Power Movement was merely a strong reaction to the sudden realization that white folks were not going to allow black people to have comfortable positions within America's technology. It was not a revolt against technology, urbanization, and industrialization. And the specific problems Black people face in America are the direct results of technological advances—advances so great that the services of Black people are no longer needed. Black people in America are not educated to fill roles because there are fewer roles than there are individuals and, as we all know, whites fill the power positions and we Black people get the leftovers. The Civil Rights Movement overlooked the need for it to teach/train/and educate Black people with technical skills before having numerous laws written. Because if Black people had been trained, then they could have built pockets of power around their most stable institution, the church, and thus been able to compete for the spoils thrown down by the rulers. The hasty and necessary steps taken to remove embarassing backseat signs were but a belief that eventually Black people would fulfill any roles they qualified for. This is fallacious thinking because there are only a few rewards, in terms of roles, in urban, technological, and capitalistic societies and the vacancies are filled by the members of those groups who understand the system well enough to know how to carve out places for themselves between the untouchable rulers and the starving masses. This is the political, economic, psychological, and cultural reality of America—all individuals fighting for what only a few can possibly get. Black people must understand that no laws, no marching, no rapping, no writing of plays, poems, or novels will ever change the basic structure of this society. And if this is true, then Black people are left with only two equally threatening alternatives; we can either remain here and join the fierce rat race where nobody will ever win and everybody will lose, or we can plan to return to the Motherland and build a strong nation for ourselves there.

But what is crucial is that the language and rhetoric of real revolution, where the struggle for land will be prolonged, has no functional place in an industrialized society where all that is being demanded is that more people be put in the distribution line while the basic power structure remains unchallenged. Example: there is no need calling a black cat appointed to the board of directors of GM revolutionary because when the people who appointed him get tired of him, they gon' dis-appoint him.

Frankly, I don't think a revolution is either probable or wise in America because our environment is controlled too closely, and resistance can be easily confined to certain areas and stymied. I do, however, believe that we Black people can acquire as much knowledge about technology as any other group if the resources (the funds of the Black church) are pooled and alternative educational systems are set up. But more than technology could be taught (things cultural, historical, etc.). This could begin with day care centers and kindergartens and glide into elementary schools. No matter what we Black people need, we won't get it as long as the white man is responsible for educating successive generations of our Black children.

People are educated to master technology and all the prayers, poems, sermons, and raps in the world cannot compensate for a good functional educational system controlled by Black people, for Black people, and viable enough to be passed on from one generation to the next.

The Black church has the funds, the property, and the leaders, *if* they stop begging Congress, Governors, and the President long enough to realize the vast amount of power they would have if they would only organize around the educational needs of the budding Black nation.

It could be that all men are absolutely helpless to do anything to alter their fate and that the only significant thing in their lives is their attitude about life. Another facet of the same phenomenon is the relationship between the kinds of attitudes people have about their fate and the kinds of things they do, or attempt to do, to control what happens to them. The question of whether all men are but mere cosmic children, at the mercy of uncontrollable forces, is the fulcrum of the Black dilemma today. The crisis we now face concerns the answers to two questions: will the Black Rituals remain tied to moral considerations of what should be done based upon spiritual laws (laws which give us our artistic identity), or will the Black church "liberate" us from their rule? For example, when the farms became mechanized after World War II, millions of we Black people found ourselves unemployed and helpless to do anything about it. Thus we left our ancestral homes in the South and sought greener pastures in the factories of the North, East, and West.

As migrants, we were not trained for the jobs we were seeking and many of us found that we didn't have the training to gain other employment. What this did for us, having been brought up in a moral system where the individual is responsible for his own fate, was to make us feel futile, tormented, and driven to despair.

The severity of this crisis is reflected in the fact that the Black church didn't interpret Black joblessness in social terms like increase in automation, technology, etc. . . . Even worse, the Black church did not have any programs designed to do anything about problems directly related to industrialism and the automating of this country. In fact, the sole beneficiary of the Black church was the preacher. He got new homes, new suits, new Cadillacs, and the people got nothing. There were no day care centers, no free breakfast programs, no welfare programs, no housing programs, no savings and loan associations, and no educational programs.

We find ourselves today in a desperate situation similar to that faced by Martin Luther King, Jr., and the Montgomery Improvement Association in 1956, when they opted

67

to challenge the legality of segregated busing by using the institutional facilities of the Black church as the basis for mobilizing Black people. The historical significance of Montgomery and all the later sit-ins, walk-ins, wade-ins, work-ins, etc. . . . was that the Black church was acting in a very relevant manner, addressing itself to the immediate, day-to-day needs of Black people. But what is really shocking about the whole Civil Rights Movement is the fact that nowhere did the Black church show any willingness to be autonomous. It presented a well-organized protest and expected the leaders of the Federal Government and the Judiciary to rectify things. The church in Montgomery should have begun a bus company after winning the right to sit any where they chose to sit.

All over the nation as lunch counters were integrated, the Black church should have established restaurants owned and operated by its Black members. Also, after forming tenant unions in the ghettos, the Black church should then have begun financing housing for the poor instead of relying on Congress and the President to do anything meaningful about the situation.

The occurrence of the riots, the emergence of Black Power rhetoric, and the murder of Dr. Martin Luther King, Jr., has increased the urgency for the Black church to do something now, other than hold protest meetings. To begin with, all the people involved in the Civil Rights Movement saw themselves as enlightened liberators bringing about justice in America. Thus when it became apparent with the rise of Black Power rhetoric and the riots that Black people weren't being freed from anything, the liberators, particularly, SNCC, reacted emotionally to a political problem. There emerged numerous personalities rapping about Blackness and culture and leading a new mass movement.

This movement found its most celebrated spokesmen travelling like members of the "jet set" from big university campus and T.V. camera to big university campus and talk shows. What this did for a lot of Black people who sympathized with the rhetoricians was to make them feel that answers were being given, when in reality what was happening was a disruptive national sensitivity session between Black spokesmen and White folks, with "Honkey" and "muthafucka" becoming the new prayers from a desperate people. There developed a grave crisis in America when Stokely Carmichael, H. Rap Brown, LeRoi Jones, Maulana Ron Karenga, Huey Newton, Bobby Seale, and Eldridge Cleaver became the spokesmen for Black people. The Black preachers found themselves out of the office of public influence. And what they did was not to address themselves to any of the problems the individual leaders were pointing out, but to hew out a position acceptable to the Power Structure and rinse their program in Blackness. Classical example: "Black Capitalism" whereby Black folks show White folks that a black face can often make more money for the white man than a white one can.

The Black church should have been about the business of trying to get land both in urban areas and in the rural areas on which to produce those things so badly needed for our maturity as a people—like schools, hospitals, farms, recreational complexes—instead of trying to get white folks to use black models to sell Kools, Oldsmobiles, Johnny Walker Red, etc. . . .

A very dangerous thing happened within the Black Power Movement when a split occurred. One group wanted Black Liberation from white folks and emphasized establishing a viable Black Culture as the vehicle to do it, while another group thought the problem was simply military oppression and thus picked up the gun and allied themselves with anybody who said they would help. For a period of time between 1967 and 1970, a vicious verbal battle was waged between the two groups. But the murder of Dr. Martin Luther King, Jr., on April 4, 1968, brought all sides to the verge of despair. For it was obvious that the powers that be were not playing with the budding Black Resistance. After many tears and the interment of Dr. King, a renewed period of Black rhetoric commenced. This time the theater was the university campus and the issues were Black Studies. Everywhere the search was on for qualified Black faculty and Black administrators.

The irony of all this is that white universities are not located in Black communities, for the most part, and by bringing more "marginal" Blacks into the university environment did not, and could not, deliver any grass root returns. What happened on college campuses was that diverse groups of Black spokesmen vied for their platforms with the students. First, the poets and Cultural Nationalists emphasized the necessity of developing a viable Black Culture, then the Black Panthers rapped off the need to bring down this whole structure now with it not mattering to them whether their supporters were black, yellow, or white.

The significance of this crack in Black unity can be seen in the way the different actors began partitioning off safe roles to play. In fact, these actors began picking the remote corners where they could be serious and contribute to the Revolution. They suffered from a severe case of self-imposed self-importance and automatically had the duty to tell everybody else what they should and should not be doing. You see these new Black prophets fell into the same trap in which Black preachers had sunk, the trap of believing that what they said and did was the only way to bring about a change and expecting everybody to follow their loud heedings. The crime committed most consistently by Black leaders is their crime of not really trusting what the masses of Black people feel.

The preachers made the mistake of not caring what they felt, and the Black Revolutionaries made the error of trying to use the language of the masses and tell them what they should feel. For instance, the only people who need to question if there is such a thing as Black Art are the people who don't know. Of course, there has always been Black Art and the Blues, Spirituals, and the Black church serve to testify to this fact. But the question raised by the artists seemed to indicate that art gives direction (not culture). It does. And if they had been brought up appreciating their own art, then they would not have needed to theologize their beliefs in certain music, certain poets, and certain painters. They would have known that, for instance, no matter how well one sings the Blues (Bessie Smith, Ray

Charles, B. B. King) that the political realities which oppress Black people will not disappear until Black people mobilize politically and there is no one, guaranteed way to bring about this politicalization of Black people.

I mean it sounded ridiculous to me for Black writers to be saying that the Black church was the only valid theater when they weren't in the Black church. For if the Black church is really Black theater then the most gifted dramatists must go into the church. There is no need for a church surrogate if the church is the real thing; that is probably one of the reasons that the church has won the battle with the theater in the race for Black audiences.

Another misunderstanding concerns the Blues. People who sing the Blues are reflecting a worldview that is particularly Black. They have not resigned to accept their fate but have found ways to admit to themselves and their brethren their troubles. I don't think this necessitates a dichotomy with Blackness. Aretha Franklin sings the Blues, Nina Simone sings the Blues, Ray Charles sings the Blues, and the Black man lives the Blues.

But the jargon born along with a cultural nationalist philosophy demanded that a new neo-mythology replace the directness and simplicity of the Blues. For example, ancient African Gods, Shango, Dambalah, Orisha, etc. . . . would be called upon. I say it makes no difference what God you call upon if you are a slave, because if you don't free yourself, you don't get freed. What I'm referring to is the fact that in industrialized and technological societies, knowledge of history and culture are fine, but what counts is how pragmatic our knowledge is; will it bring about the change now. If not, are there better models to guide our movements? I suggest that Black Cultural Nationalism is the answer if, and only if, there is some merger with the Black church because then there will be both current Black assessment and the only Black structure capable of organizing most Black people. The Black artist is important because he has kept the truth about our existence in a sort of asylum, and the Black preachers can use that truth to liberate the minds of the masses. I don't feel that Black artists can become Black

71

preachers unless they are willing to build churches. I know they have the message, but I hope they will constantly reveal the truth and let the institutions bring it down to Black people. That is the most effective way of doing it.

Since we Black people are slaves, a common syndrome observable among us is the attitude of "I'm as good as any other Black man (really nigger)" meaning "I can't live if other Black people have avenues of escaping the hardships I must face." This attitude finds its most ostentatious expression in situations where evidence points to the fact that some members of a particular family have more acumen (talent) than others have. The parents, invariably, refuse special treatment (education) for the bright child lest he become more educated and uppity and outshine his siblings. The parents' comments are "If Dunbar was good enough for me and my other chilluns, why ain't it good enough for him." The consequences of this tragedy is that future generations of Black people are denied the fruit of minds which could/should have been developed to their maximum potential.

This syndrome isn't found solely among the inarticulate and uneducated, but also among the "very brilliant" leaders of the future. Its most bizarre exhibitions simply say "If one Black man is a slave, then all Black men are slaves" meaning that if collectively Black people are slaves, then one Black who is accepted into the mainstream of technological benefits doesn't change the fact. But what is crucial about this kind of thinking, which seeks to produce a kind of collectivized psyche where "we Black people" comes before "I a Black individual" is that several separate problems are handled very clumsily and inadequately. Two distinct questions can be asked to clarify the role collectivization should play in developmental training if collectivized action is the final result. First, does socializing an individual into a collectivized psyche (diluting his sense of self) make him more functional in later group activity, and secondly, does socializing individuals to be strong, competent, and self-directing individuals necessarily make them selfish, competitive, and capitalistic?

To answer any question about collectivization and socialization, an analysis must be made of the society in which the individuals will have to survive in. Thus if we Black people are going to have to live in America's industrialized maze, then we must learn ways of thinking and doing that will enable us to survive, but do we if "no one wins" in America, not in some ancient African system.

The problem here is that most ideologies which seek to make it possible for Black people to survive always emphasize the need for Black people to think in unity, act in unity, and feel in unity, but what is lacking is any coherent explanation of what it is that makes people act in unity. White folks sure act in unity when the problem is their survival but they are trained to be individuals, or more specifically, white people are trained/developed/educated according to their special aptitudes, thus there is diversity allowed yet all individuals are taught that if they don't make it, it is because they didn't learn to compete.

What Black leaders must understand is that it is not necessary to discourage people from developing strong individual personalities in order for them to function in unity. In America, individuals who achieve must have a strong sense of self and the pragmatic belief that anything can be achieved if the right training is given. The problem with Black intellectuals is that most of the solutions they give are cloaked in the eternal truisms of religious dogma. I believe that if you know what you want people to become, then you can specify what they should experience from birth to adolescence and they will become it. But to do this one must control institutions and Black people don't control any institutions, except the Black church. For if Black people controlled the education of Black children, then the whole question of culture would not be discussed solely in terms of philosophy, but it would be practiced from day to day and adjustments could be made to fit different circumstances.

Any ideology which doesn't facilitate the Black man's ability to deal with his oppressing problems is nonfunctional. When Black people gain power over their lives or act as if they have it, then the problems of the production of individuals versus the production of one mass Black psyche won't be a question. Part of the hang-up, fear of Black individuals, stems from the fact that Black leaders are powerless. They don't have any power unless the masses follow them.

I maintain that if Black leaders seek to make every Black man as rich and versatile as possible, then they will necessarily make Black people more resourceful and dedicated as a constituency. In short, developing people who are highly individualistic, competent, competitive, aggressive and acquisitive doesn't hinder them from functioning in the interest of one idea if their leaders have a practical program for them to be incorporated into (the astronauts are examples).

The days for kings and subjects are over and Black people will opt for the kind of free choice slavery under capitalism before they will submit to the ego needs of leaders who feel that they must de-adultize them into following "true leaders." The conditioning the Black man has received in his socialization process prevents him from accepting non-egalitarian ideas. Black leaders must understand and deal with this fact. At least (in the minds of Black people) the Democrats and Republicans allow them the choice of two men to vote for. They may even discard their votes but, nevertheless, they do put on a good "democratic" show. Black leaders must do the same thing, if they are to gain the good faith of the majority of Black people.

Let me further say that to thoroughly understand technology and materialism means that one must de-mythologize his worldview (and this de-mythologizing may be tragic); it means a de-emphasis on religion. At the base of all religion in the West (and we're in the West) is a class of priests, shamans, emans, etc., . . . who decipher for the masses what reality is and ought to be. In America, Black preachers have had a monopoly on reality, but as the twentieth century wanes, there increasingly emerge worthy competitors. In the Twenties and Thirties were the Marxists, then Marcus Garveyism (really a pragmatic Black Nationalism) then Islam (the Nation of Islam has been the only group to meet both the material and Nationalistic needs of Black people), then came Civil Rightsism and Black Powerism with Black Cultural Nationalism and the poets, painters, dramatists, and musicians as the new interpreters.

The problem is that all these different "isms" are workable if Black people are unified, but the manner in which they are presented alienates the class of Black people who are needed as the catalyst for unification—the Black middle class. The bag of political programs which the Black middle class refuses to buy from all the idealogues is due to the fact that they (the idealogues) unequivocally claim all the answers, therefore all followers must submit completely to the will of the leaders. This type of thinking is found on the battlefield but it is horrible when you are trying to gain allies to make your non-aggressive programs work. The fact to keep in mind is that the most successful class of any group becomes the ideal for that group. In regards to the Black middle class, they must be made a part of any program that is to be successful because they have the skills necessary for the task before you, and for no other reason. What should be done is that the leaders should praise those aspects of the Black middle class which are good and try to modify those aspects which are negative. The same procedure should be used to evaluate all of the different economic, educational, racial, and social groups. Never should any leader adopt any particular group as the model for everybody else to follow. It is bad strategy and will factionalize the people along lines of differences rather than healing them into unity.

Because the Black middle class possesses the skills which allow them to compete within the system doesn't mean that they are capable now of leading the race anywhere; only that they must be included in any functional program. And it doesn't mean that the cat on the block is any more capable of leadership either. What is needed is a merger of the street psychology of right-now-concretism with the middle class skills of manipulation, or we Black people must take from educational facilities only that which aids our survival. I know I'm sounding cliché but after six years of Blackness, Black Power, and Black Cultural Nationalism, there still hasn't emerged any workable model which can be applied to Black people in general (by workable model or formula, I mean something similar to Judaism for the Jews or the Catholic Church for Irish-Americans).

When Blackness erupted, the loudest advocates were the sickest Black people and their sudden conversions were not in time with that of the majority of their brothers. Many Blacks who were in the forefront in the fight for Civil Rights (integration) saw plainly that integration had been merely a promise—a promise which had prevented Black people from taking their own destiny into their own hands. Thus what the most vociferous Black Power spokesmen became in 1966 and 1967 were facilitators in a National Black Sensitivity Session, a sensitivity session that was desperately needed and one which allowed many negative adjectives to flow, but which was a sensitivity session that ended before Black people grew enough to transform their beautiful raps into pragmatic actions. For Black Power had not been institutionalized yet.

Black Power began in the political arena with T.V. talk shows, conferences, and university rallies as the stage. Then it underwent a mild metamorphosis and re-appeared as Black Studies on white campuses. The problem with all of this is that it occurred outside of the Black community and it occurred because uncouth college administrators were faced with novel situations and rather than make things worse, they capitulated until the Justice Department and Pentagon had planned a more desirable course for them to take.

Today, in the household of Blackness, there linger Black people with no announced allegiances; they wear the safe personas of Blackness but deep beneath there is their personality No. 2 telling them, encouraging them, begging them not to put everything in Blackness but to sort of spread themselves out. These weird creatures are often writers, and critics in particular. What they do is to tell everybody the value of Black Culture, the Blues, Spirituals,

76

and the Black preachers, Pimps, and Prostitutes, etc., . . . but invariably they are people who have had less experience with anything Black than the people to whom they are addressing themselves. It is not even clear *who* they are speaking for, because it seems that they are trying to speak to Black people so loudly that the man will hear them and ask them to speak to Black people from his organs—magazines, newspapers, etc.—and this gives these weirdos perfect rationalizations for their actions because "the *New York Times* reaches more brothers than *Black World,* and white publishers give me the kind of advance I need so I can be free of work and do serious writing." If these niggers were serious they wouldn't regulate their roles in the Black struggle solely to the kinds of critical/creative products they can produce.

I feel that if the Black church is functional and is theater then there is no need for another theater; playwrights should become preachers and so should actors and they should stay in the Black churches. Also at the time when Black unity is badly needed it is those initial, very Black spokesmen, who refuse to sacrifice finance (money) in order to make Black institutions work, who write solely for Black presses, newspapers, etc., . . . they all publish with the Man because they need the money. Balony!

Black survival is contingent upon the revival of the Black church as a lifesaving institution, lifesaving in that it again sees its primary mission as utilizing its resources to make life better for Black people here on earth. The church, as an invisible institution, during those trying years of plantation slavery was a wellspring of hope, a forum for growth, and the major catalyst for freedom, abolition, liberation. The church played a crucial role during the horrible years of Reconstruction by offering plans, laying foundations for schools, hospitals, settlements. The point is that the indigenous Black church was never interested solely in saving souls but was interested in saving bodies as well. The shift from rural lifestyles to urban ones meant a loss in the functionality of many of the Nation-aspects of the Black church. It did not prepare its members for their abrupt entrance into industrialization, urbanization, and ghettoization. For instance, many Black people left the churches in the South and went North to other churches without the church which they left directing them to other churches, or to places to live in, or to places where employment could be found. And if the new emigrés to big cities found themselves without means of livelihood, it was not the Black church who came to their resuce but the political party; thus, through neglect on the part of Black churches, Black people became automatized into the hands and pockets of Big Machine operators.

Black survival demands that Black people take the fate of all Black people into Black hands; this means that Black churches must initiate and sustain actions needed to unify Black people and needed for Black people to survive. Today, the Black man's most desperate needs are medical, mental, and educational. The Black church is capable of meeting all the needs of Black people by organizing itself around their basic needs. A case in point is the Montgomery Bus Boycott of which the late Dr. Martin Luther King. Jr., was founder and leader. A much overlooked fact about the movement Dr. King founded and led is that the Black church organized to do something rather than react to a spontaneous crisis; things were planned. Rosa Parks could have been bailed out and the members of the churches told to obey the "laws" and avoid trouble, but Dr. King had the insight to seize the time and utilize the institution of the Black church to make life better for Black folks, lowly Black folks. Another very crucial aspect about the Freedom Movement is that it began with very simple things such as desegregating buses, and could have been escalated to ending all forms of discrimination, escalated to gaining economic power through the use of boycotts. The church was splendid during the Civil Rights Movement but the objectives were short-sighted. Otherwise Black Power could never have become an issue.

The greatest failure of the Civil Rights Movement was that it did not unify the Black church. A workable model was demonstrated but the majority of churchmen continued their rousing-sermon approach to the problems of the world.

Also, had the Civil Rights Movement produced one hospital, one grammar school, one high school, and one university, then maybe that would have been impetus enough for other churches to follow suit. The Civil Rights Movement was predicated on the belief that the country had wronged the Black man and would redress these wrongs. There were no bases, foundations, for strong Black institutions laid. Everybody would become educated and live, work, and rule together. I'm suggesting that in addition to integrating schools that Black churches should also have been building them to insure that Black children would get the kind of education needed to survive.

Black survival means educating Black people to see dangers to their existence when those dangers are not as obvious as pre-dawn raids, cattle prods, or preventive detentions. It means educating the people to their position in this country and to their position in the world. For Black people must understand that as long as somebody else decides for them what it is that they want, that those people cannot be their friends. The Black church has the capacity and sanction to equip Black people with a worldview pragmatic enough to allow them means for surviving yet spiritual enough from becoming technological monsters sacrificing their whole beings for the gain of a few. Black preachers must see themselves as men of power vis-a-vis the white power structure choking the Black community. They must grow with Black people and take their platforms and ideologies from the sorrows, joys, and aspirations of Black people. This is the biggest struggle—the struggle of Black preachers integrating Black people into a strong political, economic, and cultural voice.

If we Black people remain in the United States, then we must learn to cope with this situation; this means that we must run the risk of destroying things which have made us some of the greatest artists in the history of the world. For in order to survive we must concentrate all our efforts on those aspects of life, coping styles, styles of life, which insure survival. It does not mean a loss of identity, but it means a preoccupation with systematically learning all the skills necessary for survival; this means becoming whatever it means to be an "American" on the surface but keeping our commitment to Black people as the first priority.

The problem I'm trying to clarify is the ambivalence centered around the contradiction of Black rhetoric and Black reality. Militant spokesmen tell the people of the necessity for Revolution; a Revolution is total warfare in which everything is placed upon the outcome. But militant spokesmen are not ready to make the total commitment yet; they seem to have some vague belief that maybe the system will allow the gas chambers to spare their lives, and if the system doesn't, then Black people should be ready to die. The problem is that if a Revolution is impossible to win in America, then why not migrate to those areas where prospects of winning are better. The fact is that militant leaders primarily want Black people to organize into a functional unit. And the reality most Black people face is that they cannot win a Revolution and they are without any functional alternatives to the system for survival; this is crucial because if Black militants want Black people organized, then they must organize them around the needs of most Black people, and Revolution definitely isn't a conscious need of most Black people. The whole point is that Revolutionary rhetoric turns off many Black people, particularly the Black middle class, because the spokesmen are speaking to people who are, at least, their peers as if they were their God-ordained superiors.

The grave crisis the Black Cultural Nationalist finds himself in is the fact that if he continues to live in America, then he must integrate with white people at various levels, and this integration will not always be to his complete advantage (he can't always define the parameters of the relationship). There is no point of telling people who you must work with, compete with, and live with, how different you are from them; a better strategy would be to recognize how different you are but to pretend that you are not so different but then to act as if you are different whenever you get the chance. If the leaders opt for complete separation and struggle, then hardline Black rhetoric is apropos;

however, is it really feasible for Black people to seize land through armed struggle within the confines of the United States? If not, then we must seize it somewhere else, and the name of the game has changed. For if we are to go elsewhere, then we must master as much as we can from these houses of "mis-education" called schools, colleges, and universities, and we must do it very quietly.

The problem that keeps haunting me is that Black Cultural Nationalists have not defined any purpose of life for Black people if we are to survive among white people; all I can wrestle from their ideology is that if Black people are to separate, fight, separate-and-fight, or fight-and-separate, then their philosophy is sound. But if Black people are just going to get themselves together and gain their equitable share of power within the confines of the United States, then hardline rhetoric does not aid or solve their problems. For it is one thing to successfully compete in a technocracy where your values must approximate those of the dominant group and the moral structure of the Revolution is shot down, but quite another thing to wage total war against a technocracy. I can't see how morality plays any role in the functioning of a technocracy; it impedes what is pragmatic, practical, that which works with the least amount of investment and the greatest amount of profit returns. We Black people must understand that by staying here in America, we run a very definite risk of becoming as corrupt as our captors.

Black people, understand that the waging of an all-out Revolution against the Power Structure will necessitate the inclusion of white people, and if victory is achieved then we Black people will be as powerless as before the battle commenced. We Black people can wage an all-out struggle but it will be more suicidal than anything else. The point is that we Black people don't have to think at all if all we want to do is die, but if radical changes (for our benefits) are to occur then we must begin to think radically and pragmatically. Though our thinking must be radical, it also must remain within the boundaries of feasibility and be presented in such a way that it does not alienate those Black people we are trying to give the word to. I know this will be very difficult to bring off, but it is absolutely necessary. It may be that we Black people must accept one another on whatever levels we are operating on before we can reasonably organize ourselves into some cohesive nation. I don't think trying to convert people is the best approach; for instance, if Black people are going to taverns and drinking, getting high, and eating pork, a good tactic would be to accept them as brothers in their present states and then try to mobilize them around some concrete programs, then slowly and skillfully weave your ideology into the minds of those most susceptible until you have the majority on your side.

What I'm saying is that Black Cultural Nationalism is great as an ideology but there are many steps the Nationalists must undergo before he can bring his ideas to fruition; he may pretend that integration doesn't bother him, pretend that drinking and sexual escapades are all right, he may even say that this is the best country in the world but as long as he develops the capacity to make his ideas come true, then he has been successful, and if his ideas don't come true then he must accept failure.

Black survival demands that we Black people do whatever is necessary in order to live and this may even mean integrating; this is the real tragedy because it means that to stay here in America, we must accept our enemies or fight them and there isn't much to gain from doing either one. Our rhetoric must always reflect what is practical, what we can reasonably do; it must never turn off those we are trying to reach out for. We Black people must accept one another in some form despite our differences before any serious efforts at unity will come about. We have to get used to the fact that we can all act in unison for our common needs without our submitting in toto to each others' private dogmas about life. There is plenty of room for individuality (and individuality is not individualism) but the group must always be first.

CHAPTER EIGHT

BLACK SURVIVAL

A MUCH-OVERLOOKED ASPECT OF BLACK Rituals, the Black church, is the survival value. When I decided to study the discipline of Psychology about five years ago, I thought one could find (learn) answers to life, but I soon learned that all one can ever know is alternatives. My interest in psychology ebbed because American psychology is concerned with the white boy's descriptions and deductions of rat behaviour. He studies lower forms of life and isolates out certain biological and neurological constants; then he devises theories and methods which he then applies to human behavior. I have always felt that if the rat had written his version of what the white boy was doing, American psychological literature would be much richer, much more useful.

However, the longer I studied psychology the more I realized that psychology wasn't anything more than a way of thinking, a way of thinking that permitted one to control the way others thought and acted. I soon learned that if you couldn't control every facet of man's life then the power of American psychology broke down. For instance, if people are in concentration camps, like the Jews in Germany, facing gas chambers, and certain death, then the behavior of rats would not mean anything. What people who are faced with death need is meaning in their lives, even if they see death as being very near. Although it was Viktor Frankyl who hipped me to this fact in psychological terms, I had experienced the same thing years ago in the Black church.

My grandfather died of cancer and before he died he was bedridden for about six months and there were visible signs of suffering and sure death written all over his face. I remember that Poppa talked consciously about his end that was near before he lost his speech. He always spoke of his death in terms of what his life had been. He said he knew that when he was young that his living had been more the weed of existence but thanks to the Lord that he had gotten on the right path, married, jined church and raised a family —left a good crop of life behind him. Poppa finally conceded that doctors couldn't do anything for him and all he could do was to wait on his Maker. The occasion was sad because we all wanted to see Poppa without pain and we wanted to see him alive. Only Momma, his wife understood the trials he was going through. She was at his bedside from the day he became bedridden until the early morning hour when he quit breathing, and lay warm and motionless in the grasp of eternal silence. All the children broke out in tears, shouts, cries, moans, and groans cause Poppa was dead, but Momma took it and said that he had lived a good life. When the funeral came the preacher said the same thing Momma had said that Poppa had lived a good life and that for us living to do likewise. This occasion of Poppa's death had been my first introduction to logotheraphy but I didn't realize it at the time. People who can accept meaning in their lives can accept death; people who accept no meaning in their lives commit suicide.

The Black church and Black Rituals will give meaning to Black existence and thus facilitate our Black survival, because any ideology relating to Black survival must incorporate those aspects of Black rituals and the Black church which insure survival. This means, of course, that ideologues must study Black institutions as seriously as they quote Mao, Ho, Marx, Lenin, Osagyefo, Lumumba, Malcolm, Fanon, etc., . . . and begin to build their worldview around the way we Black people cope now, and not build it around some way they feel we should cope.

The crisis a Black man who studies psychology faces is whether he will create his own system for judging human behavior or whether he will try to squeeze out every ounce of value from the European model. And psychology, sociology, and anthropology are models, systems of logic, constructed to facilitate an understanding of human behavior. The tragedy is that if the models are untrue, then whatever conclusions you reach using them are also untrue. I found myself, as a student in graduate school, more interested in studying my professors, than in studying what they assigned to me. I was determined to write the rat's version of the story and that is precisely the way they treated me, like a rat in a hole. I was put into a kind of intellectual maze and was punished when I turned down the wrong alleys and rewarded when I remained in safe territories. For instance, whenever I indicated that I wanted to study something that would benefit Black people, I was always told that one must first search, research, and study the literature which means that I would have to consult the white authorities of bygone ages. I knew damned well, and they did too, that the literature didn't have one paragraph of studies which were aimed to help Black people. I understood very plainly that the psychologist's role in America is to study the most effective ways of making people fit into the system. Whenever individuals are "asocial," they are diagnosed, not the system. And psychotherapy enables them to cope within this system, rather than to fight it successfully. What I'm saying is that I was very much aware of the fact that my training as a psychologist was making me an agent for this technocracy, and an enemy of Black people because I was to study Black people and find out what was wrong and then let the system cure those wrongs. I'm going to study the system and then tell Black people the ills and let them right matters. The majority of psychologists work for huge institutions whose sole aim is to keep them (economically, politically, and culturally) very much the way they are, otherwise they would be working for the people. Psychologists in private practice give therapy primarily to those individuals with the highest stakes in this present setup. In other words, they help the oppressors to rule more efficiently. You don't see psychologists, white or black, working voluntarily with Black prisoners, Panthers, welfare mothers, etc., . . . telling them how to psychologically beat this oppressing system. For instance, when the Americans found out that the Ko-

reans were brainwashing GIs there were a number of classi-
fied studies on sensory deprivation which were intended to
make the GIs better able to fight America's enemy; there
was none of that bullshit of experimenting to advance knowledge; it was experimenting to find practical and applicable
techniques.

White people child-rear their children into the opera-
tions of technology. They understand how the socialization
process works; they have defined factors which impede
growth and factors which accelerate growth. It may seem
funny to hear them say "no-no" when you think they should
be spanking the child but what's important is that their
saying "no-no" has a functional relationship to how their
child will operate within the technocracy; but what relationship does spanking the Black child have to his future relationship to American technology. It is very sad to see
Grass Rooters making fun of the way white folks are
brought up because they are brought up to survive in a
technocracy. Black children are brought up to survive on
the outskirts of industrialism, brought up to accept and not
to challenge, brought up to obey, to obey all laws. When
Black children do something their parents disapprove of,
they are beaten, not counseled. Thus they are treated as if
it is impossible to teach them anything without punishment.
They are hardly ever reasoned with; Black mothers must
decide what they want their children to do in life and then
hold discussions about the relative merits of different methods of childrearing.

There is nothing wrong with understanding the effects
of toilet-training, independence-training, achievement-train-
ing, etc. . . . on the development of personality. But to
understand the child-rearing institutions in any society
necessitates that the individual understand how the larger
society works. For white folks know what function the
family plays in their children's lives, what functions certain
kind of experiences play in their children's lives, and they
consciously do the things which make sure that their children get the treatment necessary for them to later thrive in
society. They do not leave to chance that which they can

control. The Black family has not yet realized what it can do to make its offspring acquisitive, manipulative, and able to competently deal with the problems of technology. I'm aware that many Blacks do function superbly in industrialism, but I maintain that their early experiences developed in them certain attitudes about themselves and their environment which facilitated their being able to master technology. In fact, in the amorphous group sometimes dubbed the "Black Bourgeosie," I find very little difference in the way they cope with life and the way white folks of the same educational and economic backgrounds do. The point is to make-it/be-functional in industrialized societies, one must become de-humanized; one must deny all his emotional responses to life and react in the cold predictable and mechanistic ways expected of him. And this is very, very important because it means that if you know what you want to do then you can learn ways of doing it. Really what I'm saying is that if the "Leaders" of Black people opt for Black people to make America their ultimate home that this means integrating into the American cesspool of ignorance, immorality, and evil.

Black people have models, the Jews, if we chose to remain in America and build a nation elsewhere. Israel exists in reality today because it existed in the minds of Jewish children all over the world for fifty years. And the reason this was possible is simple; there is no separation between Jewish Religion, Jewish Race, Jewish Politics, Jewish Culture, and Jewish Economics. What evolves when one looks at the history of the Jews in any country is that, though the Jews are an integral part of that country, they still identify with some homeland, supporting it with the best of what they have. In the current Vietnamese War, for example, scores of young Jewish radicals burned their draft cards in open defiance, refused to be inducted into service, even fled the country all because the war is unjust, but before Moshe Dayan could give orders to attack Egypt in the now celebrated "Six Day War," these young radicals had volunteered to fight for Israel if necessary. The question I ask is why can Jews be so non-violent, moral, and liberal when the arena is U.S. involvement with another country or with Black people vying against the forces of oppression here in America, and yet be stone warlords if an uncomplimentary adjective is hurled at Israel? The reason that Jews are so functional in mobilizing their strength all over the world when their survival is endangered is that Jews are unified. There are no Black men heading Jewish organizations, there are no Black critics telling Jews how to sing, what to write, and how smart they are—only Jews define what a Jew is, and how a Jew should and shouldn't act. Jewish culture is rooted in centuries of Jewish history. Jews know who they are, what their role should be in the various countries they find themselves in, and they know what their commitment to Israel is. They learn this from their institutions instead of watching Jewish entertainers on T.V. financed by the people who are oppressing them. What is very essential to any correct understanding of the "success" of the Jews in any country is the fact that they learn to play roles, wear many different masks, in order to make it, advance in technological and industrialized jungles. This means that they learn how to act like Americans, vote, protest, etc. . . . but in their familial and religious institutions they also learn how to live as Jews must live if they are to survive; they learn this from the cradle. The Jewish mother has a special role to play, the Jewish father has a special role to play, the Jewish sons have special roles to play, and Jewish daughters have special roles to play. They are taught their roles without ever having to wonder what they should do.

The white man is taught to distrust his own feelings, his own intuitions—his own life—and trust in some formula about life. Thus white people go to various psychotherapists because they are incapable of finding out how to manage their own problems, their own lives. They are like machines and the psychotherapists are the mechanics who manipulate the parts until the machine functions properly; no mention is ever made of whether the machine functions as before, just that it functions satisfactorily. Time is important for the white man because he makes events occur when and where he wants them to happen and he is thus able to always be prepared. That's why riots in the summer are not revolutionary; they can be predicted, contained, and controlled. That's why education is so important in the white man's world because he knows that if education is done properly then he can predict the result in terms of what the educated will do and that is why many Black children can't read, can't spell, can't write; it is part of a design to control the destiny of Black people and has nothing whatsoever to do with random occurrences within the environment.

The problem most white people face in America's huge, urban, industrialized battlefield is very similar to what we Black people face in terms of real power, for only a few white men control everything. But a very important difference between white people and us Black people is the fact that the power structure has ordained it that white people fulfill the few roles (jobs, positions, functions, etc.) and that we Black people must merely survive off the crumbs of technology. Thus when white youth rebel, their rebellion is centered around their need to define for themselves what their lives should be in this technocracy but when we Black people rebel, our problem is how can we get into the technocracy and get the where-withals for survival. This is very important for it means that we Black people have no natural allies who are white—"friends" maybe—but no allies. The most serious problem facing us Black people today is where will we ultimately settle and call home. For if we are to ultimately remain in America, we will always be dependent upon the white man and some form of integration will be necessary for our survival. But if we are to ultimately live again back in Mother Africa, then we must merely seize the tools wherever they are for our adventure; thus educational programs must be developed to meet our needs.

The white man is hardly ever taught answers but ways of thinking which will enable him to get the pragmatic solutions. What I'm driving at is that technology is based upon a way of thinking which holds that all answers can be found if you develop the right methods and theories. A good case in point is Black genocide. For many generations such an uproar was made over legal segregation until finally the man capitulated and legal segregation is almost non-existent in America, but the white man knows that whether he legally segregates the Black man or illegally segregates him that the results are the same, Blacks under control. He knows that it is not necessary to "tar and feather" Black men shooting them in the head illegally; "legal" pre-dawn raids are just as effective. He knows that it doesn't make any difference whether a Black man plays in *Mod Squad, I Spy,* or *Julia,* because as long as he writes the script it is going to say what he wants it to say. Europeans are a very pragmatic people and everything they say and do must be seen in light of pragmatism. For instance, the late John F. Kennedy was heralded as the hero of the underdog the world over but in addition to having Dr. King at the White House for coffee and laughs after the "Great March," he also gave his blessings to the "Bay of Pigs" fiasco and used military might of this country to prevent Cuba from gaining defensive nuclear weapons. I want to know if John F. Kennedy, Robert F. Kennedy, etc., . . . loved the underdog so much, why didn't they place all their combined funds in a trust and use it exclusively to educate the poor? I rather suspect that they were interested in the poor as long as the poor voted them into office. A good case of pragmatism is President Johnson's singing "We Shall Overcome" while lying about the Vietnamese War at the same time. It was practical for him to sing the freedom song and it was practical for him to give the version of the Vietnamese War that he gave.

The thing we Black people have to keep in mind is that whatever the Man says is to perpetuate his way of life, his way of controlling our lives and the lives of future generations of Black people. We cannot get hung up on who among them is all right. We must keep all of the initiative for our survival in our own hands.

This means that there should never be any need for us Black people to trust the man when he is helping us, for we should never place ourselves in the position where if he does not come through that our efforts are throttled. I'm not talking about racism or superiority. I'm pointing out how people who are caught in a revolutionary situation must act if they are to get free. I say if the Chinese vanguard have only Chinese, and the Russian vanguard have only Russians, and the Korean vanguard have only Koreans, that then the African in African vanguard should contain only Africans. You may ally if you can trust them, if they prove themselves trustworthy, but any meaningful change is brought about only by the people most oppressed who are willing to move and take power into their own hands.

CHAPTER NINE
MIXED MARRIAGES

WE ARE IN DEEP TROUBLE WHEN OUR most celebrated spokesmen are fighting the Man by marrying his woman. I have tried to deny that white women are a threat to Black Liberation. I defended Black men by thinking, well, they just have biological needs to fill, and after all, white women are women, too. Now, I'm not sure that white women are merely women and that Black men are merely trying to satisfy biological and emotional needs. The fact is that Black men are addicted to white women and the results have been a kind of cultural diabetes. The union, temporary or permanent, of the Black man and white woman, is a source of severe sickness of both parties involved. Because their union means that either they have fallen naively in love and are willing to brave whatever storms as a testimony of their love for one another, or that they genuinely believe that bullshit pitch about America being a democracy with every man having the right for the pursuit of happiness, or they feel that by marrying into the opposite race they can better help things, or they are completely ignorant of the history of this republic.

To put the question of who Black men and white women should marry in a proper perspective, let me say that the solution to the problem of Black survival demands the collective efforts of all Black people. The collective aspect of this necessary endeavor means that the concern for the individualistic urges of its members are placed in the basket of low priorities. But what this does for the Black man and white woman is to ostracize them from the committee working zealously for Black survival. And one can stop right here and ask why must the Black nation accept uncritically all the manners and mannerisms of people applying for membership in it. Or to be more direct, why aren't the Black man and white woman accepted by the White nation? The answer is simple. The white nation forbids its members from acting in certain ways and have sanctions to back up its demands. But when it comes to the Black nation it is thought to be some kind of political child sucking on the breast of Good Public Opinion, unable to demand anything less it be labeled selfish, racist, inconsiderate of the needs of others—others who have the skills necessary to wield the pitchforks for Black Liberation. This kind of plight of the Black nation has caused both the Black man and the white woman to expect the Black nation to accept their union as being holy and to entrust them with the most critical of missions: politicians, doctors, lawyers, educators, poets, novelists, editors, actors, dramatists—all roles which determine the images Black people have of themselves.

Let me be perfectly clear, I'm not putting down the brother for making Miss Ann a permanent feature of his boudoir, for she may be good honey to him, she may elevate him, she may increase his towering sense of masculinity, but what is good honey for one brother's ego is bad salt for the preservation of the Black nation. There is another aspect to this problem, the Black woman. It is a fact, a law, that all nations are built upon families. You can take any of them, Russia, England, Israel, Tanzania, or the United States, and you'll find that the key to the survival of the nation is the integrity and stability of the families in it. Then if families determine the fate of other nations, the same must be true of the Black nation. In order for the Black nation to grow strong, stable families must emerge— BLACK FAMILIES must emerge. This raises the question of whether the Black man and white woman is a Black family as defined by the Black nation, for nations define what a family is within their confines, and not the individuals acting capriciously. If Black families must emerge, then the most logical procedure for insuring this to happen is somehow to get Black men and Black women together, their unions will be Black families. This is not to say that Black men and white women are not a Black family but that this decision is for the Black nation to make and that both the Black man and white woman must abide by it.

The most painful side effect of the Black man-white woman merger is the fact that Black women suffer. First, if they have married Black men they must accept the white woman, really culturally an alien, as their equals, but if they are unmarried then the white woman has been victorious over them, taking their men, taking would be sons—taking their thrones. I maintain that this is REAL, sanctioned by the lack of laws, and that at the human, personal, phenomenological level, the Black man-white woman annexations act as a sort of bad breath—social halitosis—blown into the faces of Black people and the resulting reactions on the part of those offended are natural and expected—the rejection of the offender by the offended.

When the Black woman unites with the white man, a serious question is presented to the Black man. Is he really a man? For it is not clear whether his woman is marrying a white man, or just merely a man. Only the Black man can answer this question, and I maintain, that those Black men who marry white women answer it emphatically. By taking a white woman over a Black woman, the Black man automatically says "As far as I'm concerned, the Black woman is not for me and I'm incapable of functioning for her as a man. She cannot expect me to marry her, elevate her, protect her, provide for her, and care for her." The Black woman does not ask to be married by a Black man, he asks her if he wants her. Also since the Black man allows himself to be de-humanized, is he interested in marrying a Black woman and in being a man? Here in Capitalistic America, to be a man demands that one be assertive, aggressive, and seize the time when it is ripe and this definitely has not been the Black man's mode of expressing his masculinity. His woman is at his mercy; she reacts to his actions.

If he doesn't act like he wants her to be his and only his, then she has every right to react by accepting the hand that speaks with certainty. Thus I feel that if the solution to the Black man-white woman problem is found that the Black woman-white man problem won't exist.

The reason that whether Black men marry white women and whether Black women marry white men is a problem, in the first place, is that Black people act powerless and exert powerlessness. For if we were not powerless we would just simply set up certain guidelines concerning marriage and those individuals bucking our will would get fucked and that would be all to it. You don't see any other ethnic group in America: Indian, Irish, Anglo-Saxon, Jew, Polish, or Chicano, talking about who is one of them. They all have rules which they all respect. If one of them becomes bold or foolish enough to break the rules, then the group acts to enforce some kind of sanction, either ostracism or death. But there is never a lot of rhetoric about what should be done.

CHAPTER TEN

WHAT IT FEELS LIKE
TO TURN BLACK:
AN EPILOGUE

THE PROBLEM WITH PSYCHOLOGY IS that once you leave averages and mandates concerning human nature and other truisms, that you are finally left with the individual. And what is ultimately passed off as being true of all humans is really something quite true of only a few individuals but should be true of all humans. This is particularly frightening when it comes to Blackness for it means that to understand the phenomena one must come to terms with how different individuals handle the problem, one must come to terms with himself. Blackness is a state of mind. It is a self-image one has of one's self. But before we can discuss Blackness in any detail as a concept we must discuss the Black man's developmental history. For one's history, one's experiences, sets the limits, boundaries, to his actions. This means that if we Africans in America had incorporated various degrees of European brainwashing into our psyches before our discovery of ourselves, our Blackness, then you would expect us to use various methods of coping with the facts of our lives once Blackness becomes an alternative—the only human alternative. It means that initially, before functional ideologies are developed, you would expect as many different shades of Blackness as there were of pre-Blackness. It means that no one man's self-concept will be suitable enough as a model for all other

Africans to get Black by. For in the process of becoming Black one man's health may be another one's pathology or vice versa. Blackness is a process of self-discovery, self-assertion, and self-acceptance, and takes some people longer than it does others to become.

I have never been a white man. True, there have been ghostly white periods in my life when I became so thoroughly confused with myself and Black people that I wished that I was white, but it was never more than a bad wish. My whole development was among Black people. I only learned the Man's ways at his institutions of greater ignorance. I always find myself eating with the wrong hand, speaking a certain cottonfield rhetoric, and liking cornbread and molasses. Since my home was/is Mississippi, I have always held the picture of the white man as one who will kill you with the least amount of provocation, or with no provocation at all. I was taught from an early age that one must be aware of the white man like one watches for a pit viper in its coils. Black Religion taught me patience, taught me to squeeze out every ounce of goodness from hardships, and it was this worldview that saved me. I became Black the day I decided that I would never again enter another Catholic church unless it was for sightseeing or to cop some of those gold chalices. I didn't know it at the time but the act which meant that I would never again go to Mass was also the act which meant that I would again embrace the onion sensitivity of Black Religion, not that I would again go to church but that I would carry the church within my soul, that I would again let that church within my soul roll like a prancing river. This was not a conscious choice on my part and I thought that I was becoming an atheist.

When the erupting cry for Blackness reached volcanic proportions with the introduction of the Black Power slogan in 1966, I had been trying to become a writer for seven years. My idol was/is James Baldwin because I have always felt and still feel that James Baldwin is the blackest writer I have ever read. The blackest, not the most revolutionary and there is a difference. Baldwin, alone, of all the Black writers is bold enough to parade street niggers, field niggers, society niggers, and white folks in a way that reflects the way people relate to one another in America. Baldwin is the Black church and this saves him from mediocrity. The thing about James Baldwin's work is that though he appreciates and understands jazz, yet what he renders in the form of art is what the Black man lives—blues lives and spiritual lives—and it is his rendering of such that makes him immortal. When I had reached my whitest intellectual hour, it was the work of James Baldwin that re-directed me to the blues, spirituals, the Black church—Black life. I'm not saying that I was aware that I was an African, just that I was aware that I was Black and that the things Black people have done in this country, particularly in song (spirituals and blues), rival the artistic creations of any people, any place in time. Let me be perfectly clear about one thing, a writer cannot write the blues, spirituals, and Black church without writing for Black people. What happened to me when the dynamo of Blackness began to take on a rap and look that differentiated it from Western destruction was that I became very conscious of my need to use my Blackness in a way that would accelerate the political, economic, and cultural liberation of Black people.

I didn't say that I was always a liberator only that I had always been Black. Stokely Carmichael, Imamu Baraka, and Malcolm X clarified, articulated the fact that the Black man is in a subordinate position with the white man all over the world, and that made me a liberator.

But in Black literature Don L. Lee is the most liberating. He is the most liberating because his work more than any writer in our history mirrors the changes that he went through and the changes his people went through, and the terms of his art are such that Black people respond to it the way they responded to down home revivals. Don L. Lee is really an old-time preacher using the street symbols, corner raps and the Black Position as his bibles; when he reads his poetry, he preaches, he teaches, he condemns, he lauds, he instills hope, and he warns of damnation. The problem the Black man faces today is for Don L. Lee to get a church and carry on in the tradition of a Biship Turner. After reading Don L. Lee, and after joining the Organization of Black American Culture (OBAC), I underwent a mild form of Blackness; I decided to make Black folklore the foundation for all my later artistic endeavors. I was back home for I had to deal with the Black church, Black Rituals again.

NEW VALUES
for Don

Nobody wants to see pressures of oppression
see value in values we have
see the need to unpress oppression
to release NEW VALUES

NEW VALUES pop from our actions
pop from people doings
pop from poets and people
popcorning it to artists and
sketches of their positive acts
acts like feeding hungry babies
acts like marrying themselves to sisters
acts like acting like people workers
like establishing schools in their studios

NEW VALUES is magic
only those who act their actions
can make them match their ideas
set fire to their head directions
light up the map of their intentions
with the fuses of their functions
NEW VALUES is the African Revolution
the movement of our minds and actions

We are in REVOLUTION
either we continue to sing
paint poet play and write
to audience of our chains
or we MOVE TO organize
synchronize our TRUTH,
the reality of the MASSES . . .

MASSES are most people
people most oppressed
their acts create NEW VALUES
move them to act
and they act to can their humanity
put away containers to save the world
for they are the TRUTH
and we artists MUST feed
ourselves to people amassed
not tell ourselves to them
show ourselves to them
sing ourselves to them
write ourselves to them
but MUST feed ourselves to them
move ourselves with them

NEW VALUES is revolutionary
BLACK PEOPLE picking up
spades of our collectiveness
to dig the gold of TOMORROWS
we create NEW MAN
when we move OLD MAN
from oppressions of his reactions
to impressions of his actions

I say there is but ONE VALUE
we oppressed should have
and it is our will to crush our walls
knock down valueless institutions
knock down valueless instituted
and this ONE VALUE
leads to NEW VALUES
building ujamaa villages
instilling imani eyes
making ujima hands
teaching kujichagulia feet
transplanting kuumba hearts
cleaning umoja skies
walking on the nia grounds
we black artists must first

teach the ONE VALUE
teach it with our works
and work it in with our actions
and then leafy crops of NEW VALUES
will stand tall, green, defiantly in the sunshine. . . .

* * *

for Murry

There are Deep Pillars
Dropped in Blackmen's steps.

Our fathers' days are pyramids
Under our feet
If we stand naturally.
I never saw my father stride
And my grandfather
Taught me Egyptian climbs
Big steps up calculated slopes
Of peaked Greatness.
My steps were anchors in the wind
Silent drums weeping . . .
But when they dug
For my father
I discovered the Deep Pillars.

There are Deep Pillars
Dropped in Blackmen's steps.

When we dance through
Time our Pharonic Image
Overshadows us
Yet we cannot kneel down
In the shade of our ways.
I know you are stroking
In the cosmic pond of Africa
Making waves wobble minds . . .
As you finger print
In struggles They
Linger as hip Aunt Jemimas.

You are your father
And I am mine
And there are Deep Pillars
Dropped in Blackmen's steps. . . .

CHAPTER ELEVEN

VANGUARD:
THE PEOPLE TAKE THE LEAD

THE ONLY WAY FOR ANY OPPRESSED people to move is for them to take their destiny, their history, into their own hands. In *Black Rituals* I have mainly analyzed the personal, phonemenological, and moved toward a systematic analysis where societal structure defines the personalogical and characterological growth. One's destiny is one's history, past, present and future. It is only through a thorough understanding of the past that present strategies can be mapped for a more human future. I'm a Black African, oppressed by the vicious forces of capitalism and imperialism; the only goal I have in life is to destroy the wicked forces which are enslaving me and all other oppressed people and to develop an alternative system (communal or socialist) to insure my dreams. In *Black Rituals* I did not go into a thorough historical analysis of oppression and I did not offer any scientific way to solve the dilemma.

In order to bring about political-economic changes in society, the people must be organized into political parties around programs offering real solutions to the needs of the people. This means that all the oppressed should deal with the programs and their ideologies and eventually pick the best program and ideology. This problem is never easy but it is particularly specious in the United States because the oppressed must wage war against the two-faced monster of racism and capitalism. The problem is if there is going to be a socialist revolution then who is going to lead it. (I mean we all realize that Black people definitely don't have any interest in capitalism, and are not capitalists. They are lackeys of capitalism. We also realize that all the oppressed are not Third World. But a very serious political problem is how can Blacks and Whites be organized into a functional political cooperation in order for the cruel legacy of racist propaganda to be destroyed?) I realize that the oppressed must first be organized into a party and then the party must speak to the needs of the people and not those of some elitist, egocentric, and opportunistic leader. The Black man must preserve his African heritage and must hold the reins of power which define his fate; the white man, and yellow man has the same right. Thus before any kind of meaningful alliance can be worked out, each separate group must have hegemony in their own location.

The intellectuals must utilize their efforts not only to enlighten Black people about their African past but must also give the masses of the people the skills needed in attacking the problem now. We must help organize. This will mean establishing freedom schools, rent strikes, boycotts, and communal food centers. The intellectual must give his money to collective funds so the whole community can benefit.

In *Black Rituals II*, I will address myself solely to the development of a survival party and its ideology, particularly as it should relate to Africa and other non-imperialist continents.

BIOGRAPHY

I WAS BORN TO THE EXISTENCE OF A peasant on January 30, 1940. In fact, I was born illegally as a peasant since my father and mother were not married. The little town I was born in bore the name of Clinton, Mississippi. My grandfather and grandmother reared me, my brother, and my first cousin. Since we were all boys we had to start the business of taking care of our own livelihood at about the age of seven or eight when we were given sacks, flour sacks, to stuff cotton into. By the age of eleven we had graduated to the regular cotton sacks and were even hired out to make extra money when our fields did not need attending. The thing which hangs in my memory about my peasant life is the fact that we never had any money. No matter how much cotton we made or picked, how much corn or how many potatoes we made, we were still in debt at the end of the year.

We lived about ten miles from school and there were no buses for us to ride therefore we never began school until we were eight or nine years old and could walk the distance. As a peasant, I never attended school a full year. I always went after all the cotton had been picked and the wood cut and hauled and I always quit in the spring when cotton-stalk-knocking and new-ground-clearing times came.

My grandfather died in 1955 when I was fifteen and I moved away from fields to Jackson, Mississippi where I lived to complete Grammar and High school. In High school I became an honor student because the Black Bourgeosie had the money and popularity and I couldn't let them have everything. Later my life took me through two horrible years at St. Benedict's college, two learning years in the Army, five struggling in the Chicago Main Post Office, and ten shocking years in the capitalistic, industrial, cold and Windy City. I'm currently at work on a long novel, *Superbad and the Hip Jesus*. The novel is about Black People and the way we live. It deals with the eruptive Sixties.

Nonfiction

The Destruction Of Black Civilization
by Dr. Chancellor Williams
$16.95 (paper)
$29.95 (cloth)

The Cultural Unity Of Black Africa
by Cheikh Anta Diop
$14.95

Confusion By Any Other Name: *The Negative Impact of The BlackMan's Guide to Understanding the Black-Woman*
edited by Haki Madhubuti
$3.95

Home Is A Dirty Street : The Social Oppression of Black Children
by Useni Eugene Perkins
$9.95

The Isis Papers: *The Keys to the Colors*
by Dr. Frances Cress Welsing
$14.95 (paper)
$29.95 (cloth)

Reconstructing Memory: Black Literary Criticism
by Fred L. Hord
$12.95

Black Men: Obsolete, Single, Dangerous?
by Haki R. Madhubuti
$14.95 (paper)
$29.95 (cloth)

From Plan To Planet Life Studies: The Need For Afrikan Minds And Institutions
by Haki R. Madhubuti
$7.95

Enemies: The Clash Of Races
by Haki R. Madhubuti
$12.95

Kwanzaa: A Progressive And Uplifting African-American Holiday
Introduction by
Haki R. Madhubuti $2.50

Harvesting New Generations: The Positive Development Of Black Youth
by Useni Eugene Perkins
$12.95

*Explosion Of Chicago
Black Street Gangs*
by Useni Eugene Perkins
$6.95

*The Psychopathic Racial
Personality And Other
Essays*
by Dr. Bobby E. Wright
$5.95

*Black Women, Feminism
And Black Liberation:
Which Way?*
by Dr. Vivian V. Gordon
$5.95

Black Rituals
by Sterling Plumpp
$8.95

*The Redemption Of Africa
And Black Religion*
by St. Clair Drake
$6.95

How I Wrote Jubilee
by Margaret Walker
$1.50

*Focusing: Black
Male/Female Relationships*
by Delores P. Aldridge
$7.95

*Kemet and Other Ancient
African Civilizations :
Selected Readings*
by Dr. Vivian V. Gordon
$3.95

Fiction

*Mostly Womenfolk And A
Man Or Two: A Collection*
by
Mignon Holland Anderson
$5.95

*The Brass Bed and Other
Stories*
Pearl Cleage
$8.00

*The Future and Other
Stories*
by Ralph Cheo Thurmon
$8.00

Poetry and Drama

Blacks
by Gwendolyn Brooks
$19.95 (paper)
$35.95 (cloth)

To Disembark
by Gwendolyn Brooks
$6.95

I've Been A Woman
by Sonia Sanchez
$7.95

My One Good Nerve
by Ruby Dee
$8.95

Geechies
by Gregory Millard
$5.95

Earthquakes And Sunrise Missions
by Haki R. Madhubuti
$8.95

So Far, So Good
by Gil-Scott Heron
$8.00

Killing Memory: Seeking Ancestors
(Lotus Press)
by Haki R. Madhubuti
$8.00

Say That The River Turns: The Impact Of Gwendolyn Brooks
(Anthology)
Ed.by Haki R. Madhubuti
$8.95

Octavia And Other Poems
by Naomi Long Madgett
$8.00
A Move Further South
by Ruth Garnett
$7.95

Manish
by Alfred Woods
$8.00

New Plays for the Black Theatre (Anthology)
edited by Woodie King, Jr.
$14.95